NONNA'S WAY
THE STORY OF OUR FOOD

D1288107

A Collection of Classic Italian Cookie Recipes
Angela DeSalvo & Anna Romano

KELTY KREATIONS
Kelty '16

Test Kitchen Nonnas

LE REGOLE DELLA
NONNA
CUCINA APERTO 24HRS
GIOCHI, SOLLETICO,
E RISATE
PASTICCINI PRIMA DI CENA
I NIPOTI
VENGONO
VIZIATI
GENITORI SOLO SE
AUTORIZZATI
COCCOLE E BACI SENZA FINE
ORA DEL LETTO
NEGOZIABILE
CHE SUCCEDE DALLA NONNA
RESTA DALLA
NONNA

HOUSE RULES AT
GRANDMA'S
KITCHEN OPEN 24HRS
PLAY, TICKLE, AND
LAUGH
DESSERT BEFORE DINNER
GRANDCHILDREN
WILL BE
SPOILED
PARENTS ALLOWED ONLY
IF AUTHORIZED
UNLIMITED HUGS AND KISSES
BEDTIME IS
NEGOTIABLE
WHAT HAPPENS AT GRANDMA'S
STAYS AT
GRANDMA'S

To our wonderful mothers and nonnas
who inspire us every day.
And to our wonderful children,
for you to cherish.

A Collection of Classic Italian Cookie Recipes
Copyright © 2016 by Nonna's Way, Angela DeSalvo and Anna Romano

ISBN 978-0-9951923-1-7

Second Edition
Photography by Angela DeSalvo
Caricatures by Kelly Gyoker, Kelty Kreations

introduction

When we started our blog Nonna's Way, the idea was to have a place where we could share Italian family recipes and encourage others to do the same. The response has been amazing!

It wasn't long before we were getting requests for all sorts of recipes but especially for traditional Italian cookies and sweets. It quickly became apparent that the recipes for these classic Italian baked goods were the least recorded yet the star at any Italian celebration and holiday.

Many times we have been together with close family and friends and someone will say, "These are my favourite! Who is going to make these when Nonna isn't able to anymore?" So, with a sense of urgency, we set out to capture and record these treasured recipes, not only for ourselves but for our children and generations to come.

Throughout this journey, we have been graciously welcomed into many homes and kitchens and have had the opportunity to chat with nonnas and nonnos about their recipes, their lives back in Italy, as well as their trials, tribulations and celebrations of life here in Canada. We have witnessed bake-a-thons first hand, as groups of nonnas gathered to bake for holidays and celebrations such as bridal showers, first communions, anniversaries or local Italian festas. A sight to behold!

Some of the recipes in this book are generations old, and many have been adapted over the years. We love the stories about how Nonna got a recipe from a "comare" (godmother) and then tweaked the amount of nuts, liqueur, or other ingredients.

While testing many of these recipes, we were faced with baking dilemmas such as "flour as much as needed", "half an eggshell of oil", and "one ricotta container of sugar"! We were often given just a list of ingredients without any quantities. This is why we tested recipes ourselves, at times combining different versions we received, and then made sure they were 'Nonna-approved'!

We have learned that it takes a bit of practice to get the hang of the techniques, but it is well worth the effort! We want to emphasize that you do not need to be a professional baker with special equipment to make these recipes. In fact, most nonnas prefer to use their hands to mix the ingredients so they can "feel" when the dough is just right.

We hope you enjoy our collection of these classic Italian cookies and that it inspires you to get into the kitchen with your children and make memories. We would love to hear your stories and experiences!

Happy baking!

CONTENTS

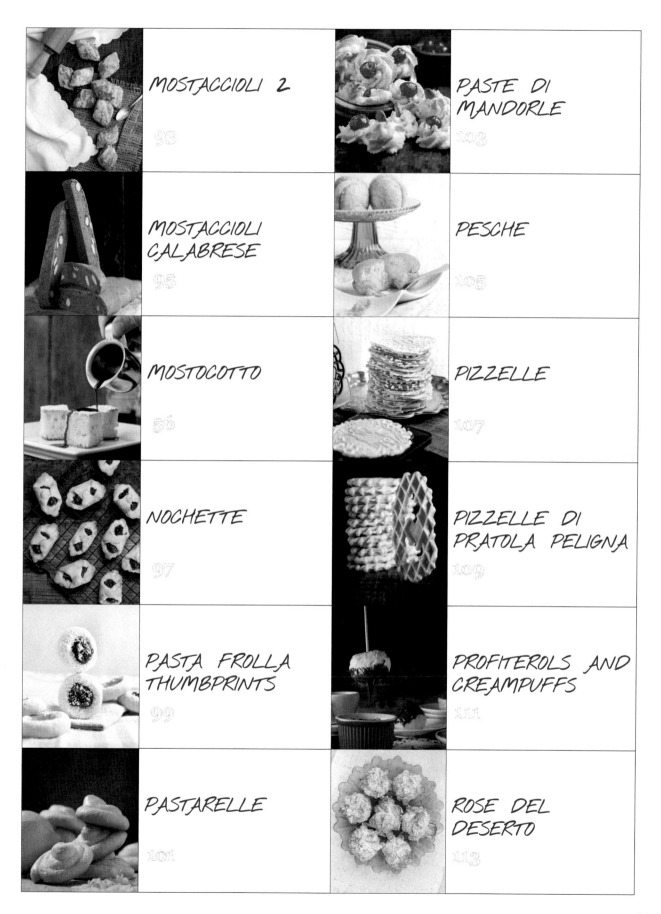

A couple of essential Italian baking ingredients you may not be familiar with:

LIEVITO VANIGLINATO

THIS IS A VANILLA-FLAVOURED RISING AGENT THAT IS COMMONLY USED IN ITALIAN BAKING. WE DO NOT RECOMMEND SUBSTITUTING THIS IN RECIPES, AS IT IMPARTS A UNIQUE FLAVOUR AND RISING QUALITY.

WE WILL REFER TO THIS INGREDIENT AS VANILLA-FLAVOURED ITALIAN BAKING POWDER.

VANILLINA

VANILLINA IS AN AROMATIC VANILLA FLAVOURING POWDER. IT DOES NOT CONTAIN SUGAR OR ALCOHOL AND GIVES BAKED GOODS THAT DELICATE VANILLA FRAGRANCE WITHOUT LOSING ITS INTENSITY DURING BAKING.

USE A 1 X ½ GRAM PACKAGE IN PLACE OF 1 TEASPOON OF VANILLA EXTRACT WHEN SUBSTITUTING.

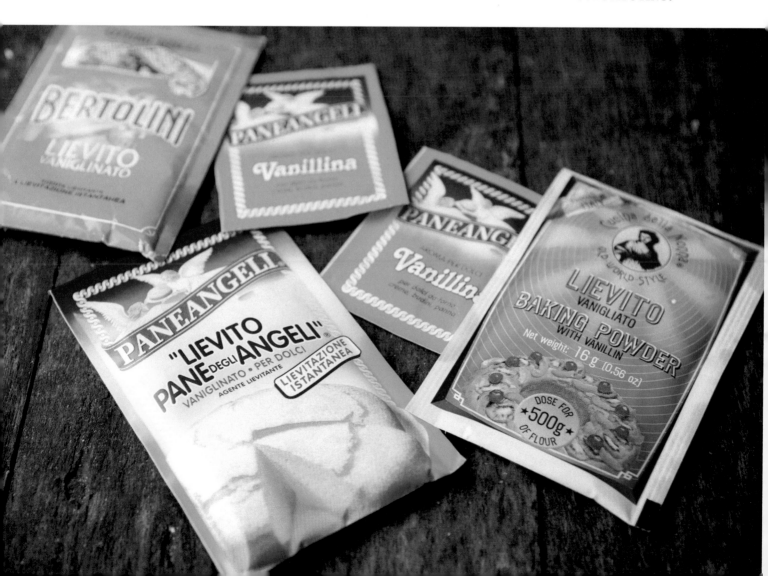

ALMOND CRISPS

THIS COOKIE HAS A CRISPY EXTERIOR SHELL WITH A CHEWY INTERIOR UNLIKE ANY OTHER. THE ALMOND FLAVOUR IS DEFINITELY THE HIGHLIGHT IN THIS COOKIE.

454g (16 oz) store bought almond paste

4 large egg whites (room temperature)

2 cups (500 mL) granulated sugar

Preheat oven to 350°F with the rack positioned at the top.

Prepare a baking sheet lined with parchment paper.

Grate the almond paste and set aside.

In a large mixing bowl, beat the egg whites until stiff. While mixing on high speed, add the sugar 2 tablespoons at a time. Add the grated almond paste and mix until well incorporated (approximately 2 minutes).

For each cookie, drop a tablespoonful of batter onto the baking sheet. Leave plenty of room, as the dough will spread.

Bake for 15 minutes without opening the oven door. Turn the baking sheet and bake for another 5 minutes or until golden brown.

Let the cookies cool completely before removing from parchment paper.

TIPS

To keep these cookies crisp, do not store in a closed container with any other cookies. If you are not consuming the cookies immediately, place in a food-safe, airtight container and freeze for future enjoyment.

ALMOND JAM COOKIES

A CROSS BETWEEN BISCOTTI AND A STRUDEL. THIS COOKIE IS MOIST IN THE MIDDLE AND CRUNCHY ON THE OUTSIDE.

2 cups (500 mL) all-purpose flour

1 cup (250 mL) sugar

1 tsp (5 mL) baking powder

½ cup (125 mL, 95 g) vegetable shortening

3 large eggs lightly beaten with a fork

1 Tbsp (15 mL) golden rum

1 cup (250 mL) peach jam (or other preferred flavor)

1 cup (250 mL) finely chopped walnuts

½ cup (125 mL) sugar

¼ tsp (1.25 mL) of cinnamon

zest of 1 lemon

1 egg for egg wash

sliced almonds for the top

Preheat oven to 370°F.

Prepare a baking sheet lined with parchment paper.

Mix together the flour, sugar, and baking powder. Add the shortening and mix with your hands to form pea-sized pieces. Add the eggs and rum and mix together by hand to form a dough. Be careful not to overmix. Cover with food-safe plastic wrap and let the dough rest while you prepare the filling.

On a floured surface, divide the uncovered dough into 4 equal pieces.

Roll out 1 piece at a time into a rectangle approximately 12X10-inch and ⅛-inch thick.

Spread 2 tablespoonfuls of the jam onto the dough, leaving a 1-inch border of uncovered dough.

Combine the walnuts, ½ cup of sugar, cinnamon and lemon zest together in a bowl. Then sprinkle 2 tablespoonfuls of this nut mixture over top of the jam.

Fold up the bottom third of the dough towards the middle and then fold the top third down over top like a letter. Brush the seam with egg wash to seal and then turn seam-side down.

With a fork, lightly prick holes through the surface of the dough to prevent the dough from bubbling.

Brush the tops lightly with the egg wash and loosely cover with the sliced almonds.

Place onto the baking sheet seam side down and spaced well apart.

Bake for about 25 minutes or until golden. Take them out of the oven and let cool slightly for about 10 minutes. Lower the oven temperature to 200°F.

Slice each roll on a diagonal into ¾-inch wide cookies. Return the cookies to the pan, almonds facing up.

Put the pan back into the oven and bake for another 20 minutes or until the cut edges are lightly coloured.

ALMOND WEDDING COOKIES

A VERY SIMPLE COOKIE WITH LOADS OF FLAVOUR AND A MELT-IN-YOUR-MOUTH TEXTURE. KNOWN TO MANY AS THE 'WEDDING COOKIE,' IT'S A SURE BET THAT YOU WILL FIND THESE ON SWEET TRAYS AT ITALIAN WEDDING CELEBRATIONS.

½ cup (125 mL) room temperature butter

¼ cup (60 mL) unsifted icing sugar

½ tsp (2.5 mL) vanilla extract

½ tsp (2.5 mL) almond extract

1 ¼ cups (310 mL) sifted all-purpose flour

½ cup (125 mL) finely chopped almonds

Preheat oven to 325°F.

Cream the butter until soft. Add the sugar and extracts and then blend until smooth. Stir in the flour gradually. Once the flour is all incorporated, add the almonds and mix to combine.

For each cookie, use 1 teaspoonful of dough and form into a crescent shape with your fingers.

Place on an ungreased baking sheet and bake for 13-15 minutes. Cookies will remain pale in colour.

Roll in icing sugar while still warm.

OPTIONAL
Walnuts or lightly roasted hazelnuts make great alternatives to almonds.

AMARETTI

At any Italian celebration you are sure to find a variation of this cookie on the sweets tray. It is a quick and simple recipe that Nonnas love to bake with their grandchildren.

3 large eggs

1 cup (250 mL) brown sugar

¾ cup (185 mL) granulated sugar

½ cup (125 mL) sunflower oil

4 tsp (20 mL) pure almond extract

½ cup (125 mL) water

3 cups (750 mL) all-purpose flour

1 Tbsp (15 mL) baking powder

1 cup (250 mL) roasted ground almonds

icing sugar for rolling cookies

almonds for the tops

Preheat oven to 350°F.

Prepare a baking sheet lined with parchment paper.

Whisk together eggs, sugars, oil, almond extract, and water until evenly mixed.

In a separate bowl, mix flour, baking powder, and ground almonds together. Add this to the egg mixture and mix well with a wooden spoon.

Let the dough rest for about 15 minutes. The dough will be a little bit sticky, but this is okay! If it is still too sticky to roll after resting, add a little extra flour.

For each cookie, use a tablespoonful of dough and roll into a ball. Roll the balls of dough in icing sugar. Place on a baking sheet and insert a whole almond into the center of each cookie.

Bake for about 15 minutes until lightly coloured and the cookies start to crack.

TIPS
You may find it easier to lightly coat your hands with icing sugar when rolling the dough into balls.

AMARETTI – CLASSIC FLOURLESS

TRULY A CLASSIC ITALIAN COOKIE. WITH GROUND ALMONDS AS THE MAIN INGREDIENT, THESE COOKIES CAN BE ENJOYED BY ANYONE LOOKING FOR A TASTY FLOURLESS TREAT.

3 cups (750 mL, 454 g) toasted almonds

1 ½ cup (375 mL) granulated sugar

zest of ½ lemon

3 Tbsp (45 mL) of pure almond extract

3 extra large egg whites

1 tsp (5 mL) baking powder

juice of ½ lemon

granulated sugar for rolling

whole almonds to decorate the tops (optional)

Preheat oven to 350°F.

Prepare a baking sheet lined with parchment paper.

In a food processor grind the almonds, sugar, and lemon zest until it is very fine. Transfer to a bowl and mix in the almond extract.

In a separate bowl, beat the egg whites and baking powder together until stiff peaks form. Incorporate this into the almond mixture. Once it is mixed, add the lemon juice.

Let sit in the refrigerator for 30 minutes.

Take 1 tablespoonful of dough at a time and roll into a ball. Roll each ball in a dish of sugar until it is coated. Place on the baking sheet and, if you wish, place an almond in the middle.

Bake for 15 minutes or until golden brown.

TIPS

If you have a convection oven and wish to use 2 of the racks, you can place one on top and one on the bottom, rotating after 8 minutes. Every oven is different, so watch to make sure they do not get too brown on either the top or bottom of the cookies.

ANISETTE COOKIES

If you love the taste of anise or black licorice flavour — these soft drop cookies with a cake-like texture are for you. Often made for the Christmas season but a delicious cookie to enjoy year round. The glaze and colourful sprinkles definitely top them off.

For the dough

2 large eggs

⅓ cup (80 mL) granulated sugar

1 tsp (5 mL) anise extract

½ cup (125 mL) milk

2 ¼ cups (560 mL) all-purpose flour

2 tsp (10 mL) baking powder

½ cup plus 2 Tbsp (150 mL, 114 g) vegetable shortening

For the glaze

1 ¾ cup (435 mL) icing sugar

2 Tbsp (30 mL) water

¼ tsp (1.25 mL) anise extract

Preheat oven to 350°F.

Prepare a baking sheet lined with parchment paper.

In a large mixing bowl, beat the eggs and sugar on high for 2 minutes. Add the anise and milk and blend well.

In a separate bowl, sift the flour and baking powder together. Add the shortening and mix with your hands until you get a coarse meal texture.

Add the flour mixture to the egg mixture and mix with a wooden spoon until well incorporated. The dough should be a little sticky but manageable.

Take one tablespoonful of dough at a time and roll into a ball then place on the baking sheet.

Bake for 12 minutes or until lightly golden in colour. Let cool completely.

For the glaze

Mix all the ingredients together to form a thick and creamy glaze. Spread the glaze over the tops of the cookies and decorate with sprinkles.

ARANCINI COOKIES

THE ZEST, JUICE AND LIQUEUR GIVE THESE COOKIES THEIR WONDERFUL ORANGE FLAVOUR. APPROPRIATELY NAMED "ARANCINI" AS ARANCIA IN ITALIAN MEANS ORANGE. TRY YOUR HAND AT DIFFERENT SHAPES FOR AN INTERESTING COOKIE TRAY ADDITION.

For the dough

1 cup (250 mL) granulated sugar

1 cup (250 mL) unsalted room temperature butter

2 large eggs

zest of 3 oranges

½ package (1 ½ tsp) vanilla flavoured Italian baking powder (see page 11)

2 cups (500 mL) all-purpose flour

For the glaze

1 cup (250 mL) icing sugar

2 Tbsp (30 mL) orange-flavoured liqueur

1 to 2 Tbsp (15 - 30 mL) freshly squeezed orange juice

Preheat oven to 350°F.

Prepare a baking sheet lined with parchment paper.

In a mixing bowl, cream together the sugar and butter. Add the eggs, orange zest, vanilla-flavoured Italian baking powder and mix together. Add the flour and mix until well incorporated.

Transfer to a lightly floured work surface and knead gently to bring together.

Take 1 tablespoonful of dough (or make larger if you like) and roll into a log about ¾-inch in diameter. Shape into a circle and pinch the ends to seal or form into an 'S' shape.

Place on the baking sheet and bake for approximately 15 minutes or until lightly coloured on the bottom. Transfer to a baking rack to cool before glazing.

For the glaze

In a separate bowl, whisk together the glaze ingredients until smooth and creamy. Brush the tops of each cookie and set aside to dry.

TIPS

For an extra orange punch, add the zest of one orange to the glaze! If you do not want to use orange liqueur in the glaze, simply replace with more orange juice.
These cookies freeze well stored in a food-safe, airtight container.

BACI DI DAMA

THE RICH HAZELNUT FLAVOUR LOCKED INTO THESE LITTLE BITES WITH A TOUCH OF CHOCOLATE IS ABSOLUTELY DELICIOUS. FOR THIS RECIPE WE USE MELTED CHOCOLATE CHIPS BUT YOU COULD USE A CHOCOLATE HAZELNUT SPREAD INSTEAD.

1 heaping cup (300 mL, 180 g) whole hazelnuts

1 cup (250 mL) unsalted room temperature butter

½ cup (125 mL) granulated sugar

1 large egg

pinch of salt

1 ¼ cup (310 mL) all-purpose flour

⅓ cup (80 mL) semi-sweet chocolate chips

Preheat oven to 350°F.

Prepare a baking sheet lined with parchment paper.

Roast the hazelnuts until fragrant and remove the skins by placing them in a tea towel and rubbing together. It's okay if all the skins don't come off! Grind in a food processor until a fine sand consistency is achieved.

Whip the butter and sugar together in a mixing bowl for about 10 minutes. Add the egg and stir until combined. Add the salt and stir.

Sift the flour and ground hazelnuts into the bowl and mix until well combined. The dough will be soft and sticky. Remove from bowl and flatten to 1-inch thickness. Cover with food-safe plastic wrap and place in the refrigerator for 1 hour.

Remove the dough from the refrigerator. For each cookie, measure a tablespoonful of dough and roll into little balls.

Place on the baking sheet, 1-inch apart, and cook for 20 minutes. You want to make sure you remove them from the oven before they start to brown so they don't dry out.

Let the cookies cool on a wire rack.

Melt the chocolate using a double boiler or the microwave. Use a piping bag or spoon to place a small amount of melted chocolate on the flat side of a cookie and sandwich a second cookie to it.

Place cookies on a wire rack until the chocolate has set.

TIPS

For a dainty addition to your cookie tray, try making them teaspoon size. They are cute as a button!

BISCOTTI WITH ANISE AND CANDIED FRUIT

THESE COOKIES ARE YUMMY WITH THEIR CRUNCHY TEXTURE AND ANISE FLAVOUR. THEY LOOK SO FESTIVE WITH THE CANDIED FRUIT, BUT DON'T WAIT FOR CHRISTMAS TO MAKE THESE! THEY CAN BE ENJOYED AT ANY TIME OF THE YEAR. OH, AND DID WE MENTION EASY TO MAKE?

2 Tbsp (30 mL) butter or margarine

1 cup (250 mL) granulated sugar

3 large eggs

¾ tsp (3.75 mL) anise extract

2 ½ cups (625 mL) all-purpose flour

¼ tsp (1.25 mL) salt

½ tsp (2.5 mL) baking powder

½ -¾ cup (125 - 185 mL) candied fruit

Preheat oven to 325°F.

Prepare a baking sheet lined with parchment paper.

Beat the butter and sugar together in a large mixing bowl. Add the eggs and anise extract and continue to beat well.

In a separate bowl, whisk together the flour, salt, and baking powder.

Add the butter mixture to the flour mixture and use a wooden spoon to incorporate. Add the candied fruit and mix to evenly disperse.

Work with your hands to form a smooth dough. Use food-safe plastic wrap to cover the dough, and let it rest in the refrigerator for 1 hour.

On a lightly floured work surface, divide the dough into 2 equal parts and form equal-size logs, about 2-inches in diameter. Slightly flatten the tops of the logs with your hands.

Place on the baking sheet and bake for 30 minutes or until lightly coloured on the bottom.

Remove from the oven. Let cool slightly then cut on a diagonal into ¾-inch wide slices. Place the slices, cut side down, on the baking sheet and bake for 8 minutes. Turn them over and bake for another 8 minutes or until lightly golden.

Remove from oven and let cool on a baking rack.

BOCCONOTTI

BOCCONOTTI ARE BITE-SIZED TARTS TRADITIONALLY MADE WITH A GRAPE OR FIG PRESERVE FILLING. OVER THE YEARS NONNAS ADAPT RECIPES AND TRY NEW THINGS — LO AND BEHOLD, A LIGHT AND FLUFFY CHOCOLATE HAZELNUT FILLED BOCCONOTTO! GREAT TASTING AND A PRETTY ADDITION TO ANY COOKIE TRAY.

For the dough

½ cup (125 mL) unsalted room temperature butter

¼ cup (60 mL) icing sugar

¼ cup (60 mL) granulated sugar

pinch of salt

1 large egg

1 egg yolk

1 tsp (5 mL) vanilla extract

1 tsp (5 mL) vanilla-flavoured Italian baking powder (see page 11)

zest and juice of ½ lemon

2 cups (500 ml) all-purpose flour

For the filling

4 large egg whites

1 cup (250 mL, 150g) lightly roasted hazelnuts

¼ cup (60 mL) cocoa powder

⅓ cup (80 mL) semi-sweet chocolate (4 ounces)

½ cup (125 mL) granulated sugar

¼ tsp (1.25 mL) cinnamon

1 tsp (5 mL) vanilla extract

For the dough

Cream the butter in a large mixing bowl.

Add both sugars and the salt and mix until fluffy, about 2 minutes. Add the egg and egg yolk and mix to combine. Add the vanilla, vanilla-flavoured Italian baking powder, lemon zest, juice and then stir together.

With the mixer on low, add 1 ¾ cups of flour, a little at a time. Set aside the remaining ¼ cup of flour.

Transfer the dough to a work surface and knead by hand to bring together just to the point that it does not stick to your hands. Use the remaining flour if necessary.

Cover with food-safe plastic wrap and refrigerate for 2 hours.

Preheat oven to 375°F.

For the filling

Beat the egg whites until stiff peaks form.

Finely grind the dry ingredients in a food processor. Gently fold the dry ingredients into the egg whites a little at a time. Add the vanilla and stir gently.

Prepare a mini-muffin pan by lightly buttering it or coating it with cooking spray.

Roll dough to roughly ⅛-inch thick and use a 3-inch round cutter (larger or smaller depending on pan) for crusts.

Place 1 onto each opening and gently push into form.

Put enough filling into each boccanotto to fill ¾ way.

Bake for 15 minutes or until shells are very lightly browned.

BOMBOLONI

A SWEET DOUGH THAT IS DEEP FRIED AND FILLED WITH CHOCOLATE HAZELNUT SPREAD, PASTRY CREAM OR JAM. SOFT AND FLUFFY — A FAVOURITE TREAT FOR KIDS.

½ cup (125 mL) lukewarm water

½ cup (125 mL) lukewarm milk

1 Tbsp (15 mL) active dry yeast

⅓ cup (80 mL) unsalted room temperature butter

¾ cup (185 mL) granulated sugar
(plus more for coating)

2 large eggs

4 cups (1000 mL) all-purpose flour

1 ½ (7.5 mL) tsp salt

vegetable oil for frying

chocolate hazelnut spread, pastry cream, or preserves for filling

In a shallow bowl combine the water and milk. Add the yeast and cover to let activate for 15 minutes.

In a separate large bowl, beat the butter until creamy. Add the sugar and beat until light and fluffy. Add the eggs one at a time and mix well.

Add the yeast mixture and 2 cups of flour to the butter mixture. Give a little mix and then add the rest of the flour and the salt.

Mix or knead for a few minutes until you have a soft but not sticky dough. Cover with food-safe plastic wrap and let rest in the refrigerator for 12 hours.

Roll out the dough on a floured surface to about ½-inch thickness. Cut out 1 ½-inch diameter circles and place on a baking sheet. Cover lightly with a tea towel and let rise for at least 1 hour.

Prepare a small pot or deep fryer with oil and heat to 360°F.

Fry the dough a few at a time so they are not overly crowded and turn to ensure even cooking. Remove when golden brown and roll them in sugar while still hot.

Place on cooling rack. When cool enough to touch, fill with desired filling using a piping bag with a plain tip.

Best eaten while still warm.

OPTIONAL
You can also make larger, donut-size bomboloni by cutting 3 to 4-inch diameter circles.

BRIOCHE

ITALIAN BRIOCHE OR "*MARITOZZI*" ARE WELL-KNOWN THROUGHOUT EUROPE FOR THEIR SOFT AND PILLOWY TEXTURE. YOU CAN ENJOY THEM DUSTED WITH A BIT OF ICING SUGAR OR FILLED WITH JAM, CUSTARD, CHOCOLATE, OR CHOCOLATE HAZELNUT SPREAD.

1 cup (250 mL) lukewarm water

1 tsp (5 mL) granulated sugar

4 tsp (20 mL) active dry yeast

6 large eggs

2 cups (500 mL) granulated sugar

½ cup (125 mL) room temperature butter

1 cup (250 mL) milk

zest of 1 lemon

zest of 1 orange

8 cups (2000 mL) all-purpose flour

1 egg for egg wash

granulated sugar for sprinkling

Add the water and 1 teaspoon of sugar to a bowl and sprinkle the yeast on top. Cover and let rest until frothy (about 5 minutes).

In a large mixing bowl, lightly beat the eggs and sugar together. Add the butter and mix well. Add the yeast mixture, milk, and zests, mixing after each addition.

Add the flour, starting with 2 cups and then 1 cup at a time. Work the flour in with your hands after each addition. Knead lightly until you have a smooth, soft dough that bounces back when touched.

Cover with a clean tea towel and let rise for 4 hours.

Preheat oven to 380°F.

Prepare 2 foil liners or baking sheets lightly coated with cooking spray.

Place your dough onto a lightly floured work surface and cut off 2 equal pieces at a time. Roll each piece into a ¾-inch log. Lightly twist the 2 logs and bring together in a circle. Pinch the ends together to seal and set on a baking sheet. For croissant shapes, roll out the dough to roughly 12-inches by 12-inches and ¼-inch thick. Cut out long triangles that are 4-inches wide on top. Make a little slit in the center of the the 4-inch side and roll towards the point of the triangle. Place on baking sheet with the seam face down. Cover prepared brioche with a clean tea towel and let rise for 20 minutes.

Beat 1 egg well with a fork to make an egg wash and lightly brush the tops of the risen brioche. Sprinkle with sugar.

Place on middle rack and bake for 20 minutes or until golden.

Remove and transfer to baking rack.

OPTIONAL

A touch of golden rum or sambuca can be added for extra flavour. They freeze very well. Thaw completely or warm them up in the oven before serving. They can also be sliced in half and toasted for a yummy breakfast treat!

BRUTTI MA BUONI

"Brutti ma buoni", ugly but good, have a crisp exterior shell with a soft and chewy inside. Not a picture-perfect cookie but packed with tons of flavour.

2 ¼ cups (560 mL, 340 g) hazelnuts

2 ½ Tbsp (40 mL) water

¼ cup (60 mL) caster sugar

1 Tbsp (15 mL) honey

2 large egg whites

1 cup (250 mL) icing sugar, lightly packed

Preheat oven to 320°F.

Prepare a baking sheet lined with parchment paper.

Place the hazelnuts on a separate baking sheet and roast in the oven until they become fragrant, about 5 minutes, being careful not to burn them.

Remove hazelnuts and wrap them in a tea towel for 5-10 minutes. This will help the skins come off easier. Remove as many of the skins as possible by rubbing them in the tea towel. Set aside to cool.

In a small pot, heat up 2 ½ tablespoons of water. Add the caster sugar and honey. Stir to dissolve. Remove from heat once dissolved and let cool.

Place 1 ¼ cups of hazelnuts in a food processor and coarsely grind.

Whip the egg whites on high for 5 minutes. Add the sugar and honey mixture and whip for another 8 minutes. Add the icing sugar and whip for a final 5 minutes.

Transfer the egg white mixture to a large bowl and gently incorporate the coarsely ground hazelnuts. Add the remaining cup of hazelnuts (either whole or roughly chopped) and gently fold the mixture together.

Drop spoonfuls of the dough onto the cookie sheet leaving at least 2-inches between them, as they will expand when cooking.

Cook for 12-15 minutes, or just until they start to turn a light golden colour.

TIPS

These cookies do not freeze well but can be stored for up to 5 days in a food-safe airtight container.

CAMPANARI DI PASQUA

A TRADITIONAL EASTER DOUGH MADE INTO VARIOUS SHAPES AND SIZES. **A** GREAT TASTING COOKIE WITH A CRUMBLY TEXTURE. THE BAKED EGG IS A SPECIAL ADDED TREAT!

5 large eggs

1 ½ cups (375 mL) of sugar

¾ cup (185 mL) of milk

juice and zest of ½ lemon

*6 cups (1500-1625 mL)
all-purpose flour
plus up to ½ cup more for
kneading*

1 package vanillina

*2 ½ tsp (12.5 mL) baking
powder*

*1 ⅛ cups (280 mL, 214 g)
softened yellow shortening*

*eggs to bake into the centre
of the bread*

1 egg for egg wash

1 Tbsp (15 mL) water

Preheat oven to 350°F.

Prepare a baking sheet lined with parchment paper.

In a large bowl, beat the eggs and sugar together. Add the milk, lemon juice, zest and then mix well.

In a separate bowl, combine the dry ingredients and whisk together.

Cut the shortening into the dry ingredients and mix with hands until a coarse meal texture is obtained.

Add the wet ingredients to the dry mixture. Mix together to form a sticky dough.

Transfer the dough to a lightly floured work surface. Knead in a little flour at a time, just until the dough is smooth and no longer sticks to your hands.

Place in a large bowl and cover with food-safe plastic wrap.

Take small pieces of dough at a time and roll into long strips. Form into shapes as shown in the picture, leaving a small nest for the raw egg. Leave the remaining dough covered so it does not dry out.

Place on the baking sheet.

Whisk egg and water together for egg wash and brush over the cookies and raw egg. Decorate with sprinkles if you like and bake until golden.

OPTIONS
For a different flavour, add 1 tablespoon of anisette or substitute the juice and zest of an orange instead of a lemon.

CANDIED FRUIT BUTTER COOKIES

THIS BUTTERY COOKIE IS PERFECT FOR HOLIDAY COOKIE EXCHANGES. THE CANDIED FRUIT MAKES THEM FESTIVE-LOOKING, AND YOU CAN CUT THEM INTO ANY SHAPE YOU LIKE.

3 ⅓ cups (830 mL) all-purpose flour

1 ⅛ cups (280 mL) unsalted room temperature butter

1 ⅛ cups (280 mL) granulated sugar

1 extra large egg

2 tsp (10 mL) vanilla extract

2 tsp (10 mL) baking powder

⅓ cup (60 g, 80 mL) mixed candied fruit

Preheat oven to 350°F.

Prepare a baking sheet lined with parchment paper.

Combine half of the flour with the butter and sugar by hand. Add the eggs and vanilla extract and mix together.

Add the baking powder, remaining flour, and candied fruit. Mix until well blended.

Transfer the dough to a lightly floured work surface and form a ball. Take half the dough at a time and roll out to a thickness of ¼-inch. Use a cookie cutter of choice to form cookies and place onto the baking sheet.

Bake for 12 minutes or until the bottoms are lightly browned.

Transfer to a baking rack to cool.

CANESTRELLI

CANESTRELLI ARE THE **I**TALIAN VERSION OF SHORTBREAD — ONLY BETTER! **T**HE ADDITION OF HARD BOILED EGG YOLKS GIVES THEM A SMOOTH, RICH TEXTURE THAT TRULY MELTS IN YOUR MOUTH. **A** GREAT COOKIE FOR KIDS TO HELP OUT WITH!

¾ cup (185 mL) unsalted room temperature butter

½ cup (125 mL) icing sugar

½ tsp (2.5 mL) salt

1 tsp (5 mL) vanilla extract

3 hard-boiled egg yolks

1 ½ cups (375 mL) all-purpose flour

¾ cup (185 mL) corn starch

icing sugar for sprinkling

Preheat oven to 325°F.

Prepare a baking sheet lined with parchment paper.

In a large mixing bowl, combine the butter and icing sugar and mix until light and fluffy. Add the salt and vanilla and stir until combined.

Into another bowl, use a spoon to push the egg yolks through a sieve. This will prevent any lumps of egg yolk in the dough. Add it to the butter mixture and mix together until well incorporated.

Sift the flour and cornstarch together and add to the mixture. Mix until combined, being careful not to overwork the dough.

Flatten the dough to 1-inch thickness and cover with food-safe plastic wrap. Refrigerate for 1 hour.

Remove the dough from the fridge and roll out to ½-inch thickness. Use a cookie cutter of your choice to cut out cookies and gently place on the baking sheet. Leave enough space between them, as they will expand. If the dough becomes too soft and warm, place it back in the refrigerator for 30 minutes.

Bake cookies for 15-18 minutes or until they start to turn a slight golden colour.

Remove pan from oven and let the cookies sit for 5-10 minutes, as they will be too soft and delicate to move immediately.

Transfer to a baking rack to cool completely.

Dust with icing sugar before serving.

OPTIONS
**Try adding lemon zest, orange zest, or ½ teaspoon of vanilla extract for variety.
Refrigerate or freeze in food-safe airtight containers.**

CANNOLI

A CLASSIC ITALIAN DESSERT KNOWN WORLDWIDE. THESE FLAKY AND BUTTERY CANNOLI SHELLS ARE WORTH MAKING FROM SCRATCH. THEY FREEZE WELL, SO YOU CAN HAVE CANNOLI ON HAND ANY TIME. YOU WILL NEED CANNOLI TUBES TO BAKE THESE.

For the cannoli shells

8 cups (2000 mL) all-purpose flour

2 tsp (10 mL) granulated sugar

2 tsp (10 mL) salt

1 cup (250 mL) corn starch

2 cups (500 mL) margarine

1 ⅙ cup (290 mL, 227 g) shortening

1 ½ cups (375 mL) cold water

2 tsp (10 mL) white vinegar

4 large egg yolks

2 ⅓ cup (580 mL, 454 g) lard

In a large bowl, mix together the flour, sugar, salt, and corn starch and whisk to blend well.

Cut in the margarine and shortening with a pastry cutter or fork until mixture is pea sized.

In another bowl combine water, vinegar, and egg yolks. Beat with a fork to mix.

Add the liquid mixture to the dry ingredients and gently work the mixture to form a dough.

Transfer the dough onto a floured work surface and shape into a large rectangle with your hands.

Break the lard into small pieces and place some over the dough. Work the lard gently into the dough with your hands. Fold the dough over onto itself and add some more lard pieces and work them in. Continue this process until all of the lard pieces have been worked into the dough. Finish by very gently kneading the dough with your hands to make sure it is well incorporated.

Divide the dough into 2 pieces. Cover and wrap each piece with food safe plastic wrap and refrigerate overnight.

Preheat oven to 360°F and prepare 2 baking sheets lined with parchment paper.

Work with small portions of the dough at a time. On a floured surface, roll out the dough to a thickness of ⅛ to ¼-inch. Cut into strips measuring 1 ¾-inch X 12-inches.

Wrap each strip of dough around a cannoli tube. Start at one end and allow just enough overlap of the edges as you wrap so that they stay together. You do not want gaps between the edges. Place the wrapped cannoli tubes with the end seam side down on the baking sheet.

Bake for about 20 minutes or until pale golden in colour. When cool enough to touch, remove from cannoli tubes. Shells can be frozen and filled when needed.

This recipe makes about 100-120 shells but the recipe works well cut in half.

For the cannoli custard cream

2 large eggs

2 large egg yolks

½ cup (125 mL) granulated sugar

¾ cup (185 mL) all-purpose flour

3 cups (750 mL) milk

zest of 1 lemon

whipped cream

With an electric mixer, beat the eggs and egg yolks until smooth. Add the sugar and continue to beat well.

Mix in the flour a little at a time. Then add the milk a little at a time while mixing.

Prepare a double boiler and allow the cream mixture to cook on medium-low heat while whisking constantly.

Add the lemon zest while the cream mixture is cooking. As the cream begins to thicken, use a wooden spoon to continue stirring.

When the cream has thickened, remove from the heat.

Let it cool overnight in a glass bowl with food safe plastic wrap covering the surface of the cream.

When you are ready to fill the cannoli shells, dilute the cream with some whipped cream to desired consistency - not too much though or it will become runny.

Fill the shells using a piping bag. Refrigerate until ready to serve. Sprinkle with icing sugar just before serving.

For the ricotta cream

2x300 g packages full fat ricotta

1 ½ cups (375 mL) icing sugar

**2 pkgs vanillina or
2 tsp (10 mL) vanilla extract**

½ cup (125 mL) roasted, finely chopped almonds (optional)

Drain the ricotta well to remove any liquid. Then push the ricotta through a sieve to make it extra smooth. Add the icing sugar and vanilla and mix together. If using the ground almonds, add now and combine.

It is best to use this cream immediately, otherwise cover and refrigerate until ready to fill the cannoli shells.

Use a piping bag with a large star tip to fill cannoli shells.

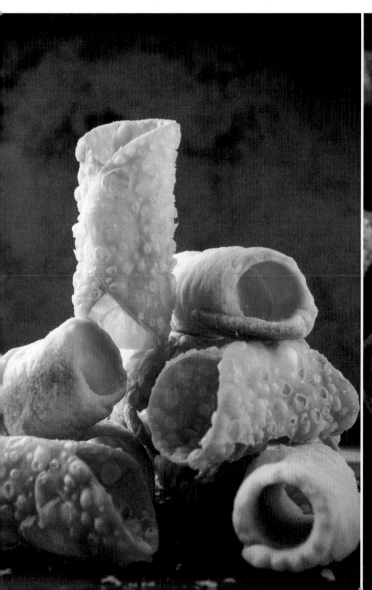

CANNOLI SICILIANI

A SOUTHERN ITALIAN PASTRY DESSERT WITH A THIN AND CRISPY OUTER SHELL AND A SMOOTH AND FLAVOURFUL RICOTTA CREAM. YOU ARE GUARANTEED TO MAKE A GREAT IMPRESSION WITH THESE!

For the cannoli shells

4 cups (1000 mL) all-purpose flour

¼ cup (60 mL) granulated sugar

½ cup (125 mL, 95 g) vegetable shortening

1 large egg

1 cup (250 mL) white wine

pinch of salt

vegetable oil for frying

1 egg white

For the cream

see previous page

Sift flour and sugar together in a large bowl. To this add the vegetable shortening, egg, wine, and salt and mix together. Knead lightly for a minute or two until you have a smooth dough. Cover with food-safe plastic wrap and place in refrigerator for 1 hour.

In a medium pot or a deep fryer, prepare your oil for frying. If using a pot, fill with oil to a depth of at least 3-inches. Heat the oil to 375°F.

Lightly beat the egg white and set aside.

Work with ¼ of the dough at a time leaving the rest in the refrigerator until ready to use. Roll the dough using a pasta machine or heavy rolling pin until roughly ⅛-inch thick.

Cut out 4-inch-diameter rounds (squares or ovals will work too) and wrap each around a cannoli tube. Use your finger to place a little egg white where the ends meet to create a good seal. Prepare several, but only fry 3-4 at a time. Do not fry too many at once because the oil temperature will drop.

Remove and let cool just enough to handle. Using your hands or even a tea towel to get a good grip, gently twist the tube while holding the shell to remove. This recipe makes about 100 shells. Fill only what you are going to use immediately. The rest can be stored in a food-safe airtight container for up to 2 months.

Fill just before serving using a piping bag to pipe the ricotta filling into each shell. Lightly dust with icing sugar and serve.

OPTIONAL

Try dipping the ends of the shells in melted chocolate before filling. Tiny chocolate chips, chopped nuts, and maraschino cherries are also common ingredients used to decorate the finished cannoli by dipping the exposed ricotta filling on the ends into a small bowl of any of these ingredients.

CASTAGNELLE

CASTAGNELLE ARE A RUSTIC COOKIE THAT SHOWCASE THE RESOURCEFUL USE OF THE FEW INGREDIENTS AVAILABLE IN THE OLD DAYS. THIS IS A RARE COOKIE RECIPE THAT DOES NOT CONTAIN EGGS, MILK, OR BUTTER. YOU WILL LOVE THE CRUNCHINESS OF THE COOKIE AND THE CHOCOLATE-ESPRESSO FLAVOUR IS GREAT FOR THE COFFEE LOVER IN YOUR HOUSE!

1 ½ cups (375 mL, 225 g) almonds

2 ½ cups (625 mL) all-purpose flour

1 ⅓ cup (330 mL) granulated sugar

3 Tbsp (45 mL) cocoa powder

1 Tbsp (15 mL) baking powder

1 tsp (5 mL) ground cinnamon

1 cup (250 mL) brewed espresso coffee

icing sugar for dusting

Preheat oven to 350°F.

Prepare a baking sheet lined with parchment paper.

Roast the almonds in the oven for about 10 minutes or until fragrant. Remove from oven and coarsely chop by hand or in a food processor.

In a large bowl, stir together the flour, sugar, cocoa, baking powder, and cinnamon.

Make a well in the center of the dry ingredients and add the coffee. Mix together and once everything is well incorporated, knead by hand until you have a stiff dough. Divide the dough into four equal parts.

On a slightly floured work surface, roll each portion of dough into a long rectangle about ½-inch thick and 2-inches wide. With a sharp knife, cut diagonally to make diamond-shaped cookies and place on the baking sheet, leaving a 1-inch space between cookies.

Bake in the center of the oven for 18-20 minutes.

Transfer to a baking rack and let cool completely.

Dust with icing sugar before serving.

Store cookies in a food-safe airtight container for up to two weeks or freeze for future enjoyment.

OPTIONAL
This recipe traditionally uses almonds, but why not try roasted hazelnuts!

CECI RIPIENI

Don't overlook this recipe just because you see "ceci" (chickpeas) and "mostocotto" (grape-must reduction)! This combination makes for a unique and flavourful filling and this dough can be deep-fried on its own for another special treat.

For the dough

3 large eggs

2 Tbsp (30 mL) granulated sugar

¼ cup (60 mL) canola or vegetable oil

¼ cup (60 mL) red vermouth

1 tsp (5 mL) orange zest

2 ¼ cups (560 mL) all-purpose flour

For the filling

1 can (540 mL) chickpeas

⅓ cup (80 mL) chocolate chips

¼ cup (60 mL) granulated sugar

½ tsp (2.5 mL) ground cinnamon

⅓ cup (80 mL) warm mostocotto (see next page)

1 Tbsp (15 mL) cocoa powder

½ cup (125 mL) finely chopped walnuts

vegetable oil for frying

In a mixing bowl, combine the eggs, sugar, oil, vermouth, and orange zest. Beat lightly with a fork. Add 2 cups of flour and mix to form a dough. Transfer the dough onto a lightly floured work surface. Knead the dough until it is smooth and stretchy, adding a little flour at a time just until the dough does not stick to your hands. Cover with food-safe plastic wrap and refrigerate for at least 30 minutes.

Drain and rinse the chickpeas. Cover with water in a small pot and cook over medium heat until soft. Drain and remove any loose skins. Finely mash the chickpeas. Add all the other filling ingredients to the chickpeas while they are still hot and mix well to melt the chocolate.

Prepare a pot for deep-frying by adding at least 3-inches in depth of vegetable oil and heat to 360°F.

On a lightly floured surface, roll out the dough to roughly ⅛-inch thickness. Use a 3-inch round cutter to cut the dough into circles. The dough will tend to shrink, so stretch lightly before filling each one.

Place 2 teaspoonfuls of filling onto the middle of each circle. Fold the dough in half and seal the edges well with a fork. Continue to fill all the dough circles and set aside for frying. Seal the edges again just before deep frying.

Deep fry the ceci-filled cookies in the preheated vegetable oil until browned on both sides. When cooked, remove from oil and let drain on paper towel. Sprinkle with icing sugar just before serving.

OPTIONAL

You can also use a food processor to prepare a smooth filling by blending the cooked chickpeas and other ingredients together. Instead of icing sugar, try rolling the hot cookies in a mixture of granulated sugar and cinnamon.

MOSTOCOTTO

"*Mostocotto*" IS REDUCED GRAPE MUST WHICH IS THE PRODUCT OF FRESHLY CRUSHED GRAPES THAT CONTAINS THE SKINS, SEEDS, AND STEMS. TO MAKE MOSTOCOTTO, REDUCE THE MUST OF FRESHLY CRUSHED GRAPES THAT HAVE A HIGH SUGAR CONTENT BY ABOUT TWO THIRDS. IT WILL HAVE THE CONSISTENCY OF MAPLE SYRUP.

IF YOU MAKE YOUR OWN WINE, YOU CAN MAKE THIS AND PRESERVE IT DURING WINE-MAKING SEASON. OBVIOUSLY THIS ISN'T SOMETHING THAT IS ALWAYS AVAILABLE, AND NOT EVERYONE MAKES WINE. REDUCING **100%** PURE GRAPE JUICE FROM THE GROCERY STORE IS A GREAT SUBSTITUTION, AND THAT IS WHAT WE HAVE DONE.

MOSTOCOTTO IS USED IN ONLY A COUPLE OF RECIPES IN THIS BOOK, BUT ONCE YOU TASTE IT WE ARE SURE YOU WILL WANT TO TRY USING IT AS A SWEETENER OR ADDED FLAVOUR IN OTHER RECIPES. WE EXPERIMENTED WITH THE DOUGH FROM THE CECI RIPIENI AND CAME UP WITH THESE GREAT DOUGH FRIES. DIPPING THEM IN THE MOSTOCOTTO ADDED A WONDERFUL FLAVOUR! DON'T STOP THERE, TRY THE MOSTOCOTTO DRIZZLED OVER APPETIZERS, SALADS, FRUIT, ICE CREAM, WAFFLES — YOU GET THE IDEA!

CHOCOLATE CRINKLE COOKIES

THIS IS ANOTHER POPULAR COOKIE FOUND IN MANY ITALIAN HOMES. DON'T BE SHY WITH THE ICING SUGAR. GIVE THE DOUGH BALLS A GOOD ROLL IN IT SO YOU GET GOOD CRINKLES IN THE COOKIE. WHO DOESN'T LOVE DOUBLE CHOCOLATE!

2 ½ cups (625 mL) all-purpose flour

½ cup (125 mL, 95 g) vegetable shortening (softened, but not melted)

1 cup (250 mL) granulated sugar

½ cup (125 mL) cocoa powder

1 ½ tsp (7.5 mL) ground cinnamon

2 tsp (10 mL) baking powder

2 large eggs

1 cup (250 mL) milk (warmed, but not hot)

½ cup (125 mL) semi-sweet chocolate chips

½ cup (125 mL) chopped walnuts (optional)

icing sugar to roll cookies in

Preheat oven to 360°F.

Prepare a baking sheet lined with parchment paper.

In a large bowl, mix the flour and softened vegetable shortening very well, until smooth.

Mix the sugar, cocoa, cinnamon, and baking powder into the flour mixture by hand.

Beat the eggs lightly with a fork. Add them to the mixture and stir to combine. Then add the milk and mix together.

Finally, add the chocolate chips and walnuts if using.

Leave dough to rest for 10 minutes.

Prepare a generous amount of icing sugar in a bowl or platter, making sure there are no lumps. Place a small amount of vegetable oil in a bowl and set aside.

Moisten your hands with a little oil, and roll the dough into 1-inch diameter balls.

Drop cookies into the icing sugar a few at a time and roll to evenly coat.

Place cookies on the baking sheet, about 2-inches apart.

Bake for 10-12 minutes. Remove from the oven and let the cookies cool before transferring them to a baking rack.

TIPS

This dough is quite sticky, but don't keep adding flour! Putting the dough in the freezer for the resting period makes them much easier to roll.

CIAMBELLETTE DI VINO

DEFINITELY A CLASSIC ITALIAN COOKIE. CIAMBELLETTE ARE A PERFECT COFFEE-DUNKING COOKIE BUT GREAT ON THEIR OWN FOR A SNACK AS WELL. THERE IS A SUBTLE HINT OF LEMON IN THESE COOKIES, AND THE COARSE SUGAR ADDS A NICE CRUNCH.

1 cup (250 mL) vegetable oil

1 cup (250 mL) granulated sugar

4 ½ tsp (22.5 mL) sambuca liqueur

3 large eggs

4 tsp (20 mL) vanilla extract

1 cup (250 mL) white wine

zest of 1 ½ lemons

1 tsp (5 mL) salt

4 ½ tsp (22.5 mL) baking powder

4 ⅔ cups (1160 mL) all-purpose flour

1 egg for egg wash

coarse white sprinkling sugar

Preheat oven to 360°F.

Prepare a baking sheet lightly buttered and dusted with flour.

In a large bowl, mix together the oil, sugar, and sambuca until well blended.

Beat the eggs with a fork in a small bowl. Add the eggs and vanilla to the oil mixture and continue to whisk. Mix in the white wine, lemon zest, salt, and baking powder.

Add 2 cups of the flour to the liquid mixture and mix with a spatula. Add another 2 cups of flour and mix well.

Transfer dough onto a lightly floured work surface and gently knead for about 30 seconds to form into a ball. Cover and let the dough rest for 10 minutes. If it is too sticky to roll after resting, add the remaining flour, a little at a time, while gently kneading just until it no longer sticks to your hands.

Take a small piece of dough at a time to form a log that is 6-inches long and ½-inch wide. Shape into a circle then overlap the ends by ½-inch and lightly pinch together to seal. Keep prepared cookies on a floured surface. Cover unused dough with food-safe plastic wrap.

Beat an egg well with a fork and brush the top of each cookie. Sprinkle with coarse white sugar.

Place the cookies onto the baking sheet. Leave at least 1-inch between them. They approximately double in size while baking.

Bake until golden brown. Adjust the size of the ciambellette to your liking.

CIAMBELLETTE DI VINO 2

SMALL VARIATIONS IN THIS RECIPE RESULT IN COMPLETELY DIFFERENT TASTING CIAMBELLETTE. GOES TO SHOW HOW RECIPES IN ITALY CAN VARY FROM TOWN TO TOWN—JUST LIKE THEIR DIALECT!

1 cup (250 mL) granulated sugar

1 cup (250 mL) white wine

1 cup (250 mL) oil (vegetable or canola)

1 heaping tsp (7 mL) baking powder

3 cups (750 mL) all-purpose flour

extra granulated sugar in a flat plate for coating the tops of the cookies

Preheat oven to 380°F.

Prepare a baking sheet coated with cooking spray.

With the exception of the flour and the extra sugar, mix all the ingredients together and blend well.

Slowly incorporate the flour to form a dough, which should be just softer than a pizza dough.

Lightly flour a work surface.

Break off a golf-ball-sized piece of dough at a time. Leave remaining dough covered with food-safe plastic wrap.

Roll out each piece of dough to form a 6-inch log, shape into a circle, and lightly pinch to close at the seam.

Turn the cookie upside down into the plate of sugar and flatten gently to allow sugar to lightly coat the top.

Place the cookie sugar-side up on the baking sheet.

Bake for about 20 minutes or until browned all around. This version of ciambellette results in a more crunchy texture as compared to the previous recipe.

COCONUT DROPS

THESE COOKIES ARE A GO-TO NOT ONLY AT CHRISTMAS BUT FOR ANY FESTIVE OCCASION SUCH AS BRIDAL SHOWERS AND WEDDING RECEPTIONS. THIS IS LIKE A SHORTBREAD COOKIE WRAPPED IN TOASTED COCONUT!

2 cups (500 mL) unsalted room temperature butter

1 ¼ cups (310 mL) icing sugar

4 large egg yolks

pinch of salt

3 ½ - 4 cups (875-1000 mL) all-purpose flour

4 large egg whites

shredded coconut for coating

maraschino cherries (cut into quarters)

Preheat oven to 350°F.

Prepare a baking sheet lined with parchment paper.

Cream the butter then add the icing sugar and blend well.

Add the egg yolks and mix well.

In a separate bowl, whisk the salt and flour together. Add to the batter a little at a time.

With a fork, beat the egg whites in a separate shallow bowl until frothy.

Take 1 tablespoonful of dough at a time and shape into a ball. Roll each one in the egg whites and then roll in the coconut.

Place on the baking sheet then press a maraschino cherry quarter into the center of each cookie.

Bake for 20 minutes.

CORNETTI RIPIENI

THIS COOKIE VERSION OF THE CORNETTO IS AN IMPRESSIVE & DELICIOUS TREAT! IT IS A SIMPLE COOKIE DOUGH THAT IS FOLDED, ROLLED, AND TYPICALLY FILLED WITH PRESERVES. FOR A SPECIAL TREAT, TRY FILLING THEM WITH CHOCOLATE HAZELNUT SPREAD OR CHOCOLATE CHIPS!

3 cups (750 mL) all-purpose flour

3 Tbsp (45 mL) granulated sugar

½ cup (125 mL) butter cut into small cubes

3 large egg yolks

½ cup (125 mL) plain yogurt

zest of 1 lemon

1 tsp (5 mL) ground cinnamon

preserves for filling

Preheat oven to 360°F.

Prepare a baking sheet lined with parchment paper.

In a large mixing bowl, stir together the flour and sugar. Add the butter, and use your hands or a pastry cutter to mix until a crumbly mixture is formed. Add the egg yolks one at a time, mixing to combine after each. Next add the yogurt, lemon zest, and cinnamon. Continue to mix until the dough comes together.

Transfer the dough onto a lightly floured work surface and knead by hand for a couple of minutes. Add a touch more flour if the dough is too sticky to handle. Form into a ball and cover with food-safe plastic wrap. Place in refrigerator for 30 minutes.

Remove the dough from the refrigerator and cut in half. Roll out a large rectangle about ⅟₁₆-inch thick and cut into 4-inch squares. Place a teaspoonful of filling in the middle of a square and then fold in half to form a triangle. Pinch around the edges to seal and roll into a croissant shape. Place the cookies on the baking sheet seam side down.

Bake for 15 minutes or until they just start to turn golden. Transfer to a baking rack to cool. Dust with icing sugar before serving.

OPTIONAL

Like many of the recipes in this book, we just had to try them with chocolate hazelnut spread, and this one is definitely a winner! These cookies freeze well in an airtight container.

CRESPELLE

FOR DESSERT OR JUST A SNACK. THIS PILLOWY SOFT DOUGH WITH RAISINS IS DEEP-FRIED UNTIL GOLDEN BROWN THEN ROLLED IN SUGAR WHILE STILL WARM. GUARANTEED YOU CAN'T EAT JUST ONE!

2 tsp (10 mL) granulated sugar

1 cup (250 mL) lukewarm water

1 tsp (5 mL) active dry yeast

2 large white potatoes boiled, well mashed and cooled

3 large eggs slightly beaten

¼ cup (60 mL) room temperature butter

4 tsp (20 mL) vegetable oil

1 tsp (5 mL) salt

11 cups (2750 mL) all-purpose flour

1 cup (250 mL) raisins (optional)

1 ½ to 2 cups (375-500 mL) lukewarm water

vegetable oil for deep frying

white granulated sugar for rolling

Dissolve 2 teaspoonfuls of sugar into 1 cup of lukewarm water. Add the yeast and stir to dissolve. Set aside until it starts to foam.

In a large bowl, mix together the cooled mashed potatoes, eggs, butter, and 4 teaspoonfuls of vegetable oil.

Add the prepared yeast mixture.

Mix together the salt and flour. Add to the potato mixture. Finally, along with the yeast mixture add the raisins at this time if using.

Mix all the ingredients together to form a dough. While constantly beating the dough with your hands by grabbing and lifting it, add the water a little at a time. You want to continue this for about 10 minutes until you have a very uniform, soft and sticky dough. You may or may not use all of the water.

Cover the dough with food-safe plastic wrap and let it rest until it has doubled in size. Beat it down, cover, and set aside until it doubles in size again.

Pour vegetable oil into a deep pan or large pot to a depth of about 3 inches. Heat the oil to 350°F.

Lightly grease your hands before grabbing a small quantity of dough. Slightly stretch it out lengthwise and then very carefully place into the hot oil. Turn the crespelle a couple of times and cook until they are deep golden in colour and have puffed up. This will take about 2 minutes. Cook only 3 or 4 at a time depending on the size of the crespelle and the size of the pan.

Once they are cooked, remove them with a slotted spoon, letting any oil drain back into the pan, then place them onto a pan lined with paper towels.

While still warm, roll them in sugar and place on a platter for serving.

CRESPELLE 2

ALTHOUGH SIMILAR IN TEXTURE AND TASTE, THESE CRESPELLE DO NOT CONTAIN EGGS NOR POTATOES. A DEEP-FRIED SWEET DOUGH WITH RAISINS THAT IS ROLLED IN SUGAR WHILE STILL WARM. BEST ENJOYED FRESH.

½ cup (125 mL) lukewarm water

½ tsp (2.5 mL) granulated sugar

1 envelope (2 ¼ tsp, 11 mL) active dry yeast

1 ½ cups (375 mL) milk

1 ½ tsp (7.5 mL) unsalted room temperature butter

4 cups (1000 mL) all-purpose flour

1 Tbsp (15 mL) canola oil

1 tsp (5 mL) salt

raisins, quantity to your liking

oil for deep frying

sugar for rolling

In a small bowl, mix the water and sugar together. Sprinkle the yeast on top and cover for 5-10 minutes.

Warm the milk and butter together over low heat just enough to melt the butter.

In the bowl of a stand mixer, add the flour and make a well. To the center of the well, add the yeast mixture, milk/butter mixture, 1 tablespoon of oil, and salt. Use a spatula to gently blend together the ingredients in the well. Slowly incorporate the flour. As soon as the dough comes together, use the dough hook attachment to mix the dough for 3-4 minutes.

Add the raisins and let the dough rest in the bowl for 10 minutes. Mix for another 20 seconds to evenly distribute the raisins.

Place in an oiled bowl and cover with a clean cloth.

Let the dough rise until doubled in size and then punch it down to deflate.

Lightly oil two large baking pans. With oiled hands, take a small handful of dough at a time, stretch it out slightly and place on the pan. Once one pan is filled, cover it with food-safe plastic wrap and let rise for 10-15 minutes. Take each piece of dough and stretch it again to form a log while giving it a half twist and place it on the other oiled pan. Let them rest while the oil is heating up.

Prepare a deep pan with oil for frying to a depth of 3-inches and heat on medium-high to 350°F. Carefully place 3 to 4 dough logs at a time into the hot oil. Cook on one side until golden then turn over. Total cooking time is about 2 minutes.

Line a collander with paper towels and stand the cooked crespelle on end to drain. While still warm, roll each one in a plate of sugar.

Finished size is about 6-inches long by 1 ½-inches in diameter.

CROSTATA CON LE NOCE

THIS CROSTATA RECIPE IS A COMBINATION OF JAM SANDWICHED BETWEEN TWO LAYERS OF DOUGH AND TOPPED OFF WITH A CRUNCHY AND SWEET WALNUT MIXTURE. A GREAT TASTING COOKIE THAT STAYS MOIST AND FLAVOURFUL.

For the crust

5 cups (1250 mL) all-purpose flour

2 ½ cups (625 mL) granulated sugar

zest of 1 lemon

1 cup (250 mL, 190 g) vegetable shortening
plus extra to grease the pan

5 large eggs + 1 for egg wash

1 Tbsp (15 mL) vanilla extract or 3 pkgs vanillina

1 pkg (16gm) vanilla-flavoured Italian baking powder (see page 11)

½ cup (125 mL) milk

4 tsp (20 mL) baking powder

canola oil for greasing

For the filling

¼ cup (60 mL) golden rum

500 mL jar of either peach or apricot jam

For the topping

2 cups (500 mL) finely chopped walnuts

½ cup (125 mL) granulated sugar

canola oil for greasing

Preheat oven to 375°F. Prepare a 15 inch X 21 inch baking pan by lightly greasing the pan and sides with some shortening.

Mix flour, sugar and lemon zest together on a work surface or in a large bowl and make a well. Put the shortening into the well and mix by hand until it resembles coarse meal. Form a well again and break the eggs into the center. Add the vanilla extract or vanillina, vanilla-flavoured Italian baking powder, milk, and baking powder to the eggs. Blend the ingredients in the well together by hand and slowly incorporate with the flour/shortening mixture by drawing in a little at a time from the sides. Mix gently with your hands until a dough forms. Spread a small amount of oil onto the work surface to keep the dough from sticking. Knead the dough gently by hand for approximately 1 minute and then divide in half.

Lay a piece of parchment paper that measures 15 X 21 inches onto work surface. Very lightly grease the paper and rolling pin with a small amount of oil.

Roll the dough onto the parchment paper so that it fits evenly. Use pieces of dough to patch any holes.

Grasp the long end of the dough-covered paper and carefully flip it dough side down into the greased pan. Carefully peel back the paper from the dough.

Combine the rum with the jam and stir until completely mixed. Spread this onto the dough right to the edges. Mix the walnuts and sugar together and use ¾ of this mixture to cover the jam layer.

Roll out the other half of the dough in the same manner as the first and flip onto the jam/nut covered layer in the pan. Gently release the paper from the dough.

Beat the extra egg with a fork and brush over the top layer of dough. Sprinkle the remaining sugar/nut mixture over the top of the crostata.

Pierce the top of the crostata all over with a fork. The holes will not be visible once it is baked.

Bake on the middle rack for about 15 minutes or until golden brown. Let cool and cut into squares.

CROSTATA WITH JAM

CROSTATA IS A VERY EASY DESSERT TO PREPARE AND A CLASSIC ITALIAN SWEET.
USE DIFFERENT JAMS WITHIN THE SAME CROSTATA TO GIVE SOME FLAVOUR OPTIONS. IT LOOKS
GREAT ON A COOKIE TRAY TOO!

4 large eggs

1 ⅙ cup (290 mL, 227 g) vegetable shortening

1 ¼ cups (310 mL) granulated sugar

1 cup (250 mL) milk

1 Tbsp (15 mL) baking powder

2 Tbsp (30 mL) sambuca liqueur (optional)

zest of 1 lemon

4 cups (1000 mL) all-purpose flour

1 cup (250 mL) jam

Preheat oven to 380°F.

Prepare a 12-inch rimmed circular pan lined with parchment paper.

Use an electric mixer to mix together all the ingredients except for the flour and jam. Then with the mixer on low, slowly add in the flour until a dough forms.

Place the dough onto a lightly floured work surface and roll it out to fit the pan.

Leave enough dough to form strips to place over the jam.

Spread the jam evenly over the dough.

Roll out the remaining dough and cut ½-inch strips with a pastry cutter. Carefully place the strips over the jam to form a lattice.

Bake for about 18-20 minutes until crust is a nice golden colour.

CROSTOLI

CROSTOLI ARE A DEEP-FRIED SWEET DOUGH WITH A DELICATE TEXTURE. ONE RECIPE YIELDS QUITE A FEW, AND GENTLY LAYERED THEY MAKE A VERY IMPRESSIVE COOKIE TRAY. A PASTA ROLLING MACHINE IS REQUIRED TO MAKE THESE COOKIES.

4 large eggs separated

1 Tbsp (15 mL) vanilla extract

zest of ½ lemon

zest of ½ orange

5 Tbsp (75 mL) granulated sugar

⅛ cup (30 mL) unsalted room temperature butter

pinch of salt

½ tsp (2.5 mL) baking powder

2 ½ cups (625 mL) all-purpose flour

canola or vegetable oil for frying

Beat the egg whites until firm and set aside.

In a large bowl mix the egg yolks, vanilla, lemon and orange zests, sugar, butter, salt, and baking powder and beat lightly just until mixed.

Gently fold the beaten egg whites into the mixture just until incorporated.

Begin adding the flour and work it in with your hands until a dough forms.

Gently and briefly knead the dough on a lightly floured surface until the dough has a smooth and soft consistency. Try not to overwork the dough. It should be a little firmer than gnocchi dough but not as firm as pasta dough.

Working with a small piece of dough at a time, use a pasta machine to roll it out. Pass the dough through each of the settings, thickest to thinnest, to form long sheets.

Place the sheet of dough on your work surface and with a knife or pastry cutter, cut the sheet into 3-inch wide strips. Make 1-3 small slits in the center of each strip.

Prepare a deep pan or large pot for deep frying with 3-inches of oil. Let the oil heat to 350°F. The oil is ready when the dough sizzles and rises to the top immediately. Place 2-3 crostoli at a time into the oil and fry for about 30 seconds. Carefully turn them over and fry for another 30 seconds or until lightly coloured. Use a large slotted spoon to remove them from the oil and transfer them to a large pan lined with paper towels. Allow to cool completely.

Sprinkle with icing sugar immediately before serving.

These keep well in a container between parchment paper. Do not cover or freeze.

CUCCIDATI

THIS IS A COOKIE TRADITIONALLY FOUND IN THE SOUTHERN PARTS OF ITALY WHERE FIGS AND NUTS GROW ABUNDANTLY AND ARE PRESERVED FOR THE WINTER. IN THE OLD DAYS, YOU WERE LUCKY IF YOU GOT THESE AS A CHRISTMAS TREAT. WITH ALL THE INGREDIENTS INVOLVED, IT WAS NOT AFFORDABLE TO MAKE ON A REGULAR BASIS.

For the dough

2 ½ cups (625 mL) all-purpose flour

¾ cup (185 mL) granulated sugar

1 tsp (5 mL) baking powder

pinch of salt

½ cup (125 mL) unsalted butter or shortening

2 large eggs plus 1 yolk

½ tsp (2.5 mL) vanilla extract

2 Tbsp (30 mL) cold water

For the filling

227 grams dry figs

½ cup (125 mL) raisins

½ cup (125 mL, 75g) hazelnuts

3 Tbsp (45 mL) honey

2 Tbsp (30 mL) jam of choice

zest and juice of 1 small orange

2 Tbsp (30 mL) granulated sugar

2 Tbsp (30 mL) water

Combine the flour, sugar, baking powder, and salt in a large bowl and stir together.

Cube the butter and add it to the bowl. Mix with your hands until crumbly.

Add the eggs, vanilla, and water and mix until you have a soft, smooth dough. You can add a bit of flour if it is too sticky but only enough so that it does not stick to your hands.

Once you have a smooth dough, bring it together into a flattened disc. Cover with food-safe plastic wrap and place in refrigerator for at least 1 hour. It can stay overnight if you want to make it a day ahead.

Preheat oven to 375°F and prepare a baking sheet lined with parchment paper.

Prepare the filling by mixing all the ingredients in a food processor until you have a fine crumbly texture.

Remove the dough from the refrigerator and cut into 4 equal portions. Work with 1 portion at a time and keep the rest refrigerated.

For the classic crescent shape cookie, roll out a long rectangle of dough to ⅛-inch thickness and 1 ½-inches wide. Place a thin row of filling in the center of the rectangle lengthwise. Forming a thin log with the filling helps to keep an even amount of filling across the dough.

Fold the pastry over the filling to form a long log. The pastry edges should overlap by ½-inch. Roll the log gently to seal the seam.

With a very sharp knife cut into 2-inch pieces. Gently shape each into a crescent with your thumbs and cut slits on the outer curve. Or you can cut into diamonds by cutting the log on an angle.

Bake for 15 minutes or until lightly golden.

OPTIONAL

Try different nuts in the filling such as walnuts or almonds. It is common to add a little rum or orange-flavoured liqueur to the mixture as well. Try drizzling a simple glaze over the cookie or dust with icing sugar before serving.

FRAPPE

FRAPPE ARE THIN, CRISPY, AND LIGHT AS AIR WHEN YOU BITE INTO THEM, AND HONESTLY, YOU COULD EAT SEVERAL BECAUSE THEY TASTE SOOOOO GOOD! THERE'S SOMETHING ABOUT THAT SPRINKLE OF ICING SUGAR — IT'S JUST NOT THE SAME WITHOUT IT! YOU WILL NEED A PASTA ROLLING MACHINE TO MAKE THESE COOKIES.

4 large eggs

1 tsp (5 mL) dark rum

½ tsp (2.5 mL) vanilla extract

2 ⅓ cups (580 mL) all-purpose flour

4 tsp (20 mL) granulated sugar

½ tsp (2.5 mL) baking powder

zest of 1/4 lemon

pinch of salt

vegetable oil for deep frying

Remove one egg white and discard. In a bowl, beat the remaining eggs and yolk slightly with a fork. Add the beaten eggs, rum, and vanilla together in a bowl and mix well.

In a separate bowl, add the flour, sugar, baking powder, lemon zest, and salt together. Stir to mix well.

Transfer the flour mixture onto a clean work surface and form a well in the middle. Add the egg mixture to the well. With your hands, begin mixing the flour mixture into the egg mixture starting from inside the well and work out being careful not to break the walls of the well.

When everything is combined, keep scraping the board and kneading so as to bring everything together into a log of dough.

Knead the dough using the palm of your hands to roll it forward. As the log gets longer, fold it into thirds onto itself and continue kneading and repeating this process for about 10 minutes until the dough is smooth and uniform in consistency. It should be a stiff dough that does not spring back much when indented with your finger.

You can cut the dough into more manageable size logs. Cover each log with food-safe plastic wrap and let rest for 15 minutes. Knead again for another 5 minutes and let the dough rest covered over night.

When ready, cut the dough into small pieces. We used 100g per piece, but you can use less if you would like smaller frappe. Keep the rest of the dough covered at all times.

You are going to work the dough through a pasta rolling machine as you would when making pasta dough. Start at the thickest setting and pass the dough through each of the settings ending with the thinnest. This step is most important to get that thin, crispy texture.

You will now have a long sheet of dough. Lay this flat on your work surface and, with a fancy edged pastry cutter, cut the sheet into 3 long ribbons.
You are going to form a rosette shape with each of the ribbons of dough by forming them into a circle and pinching the edges of the dough together as in the photos.

Cover the completed rosettes with food-safe plastic wrap until ready to deep fry. If you are working alone, work in batches so that the rosettes do not dry out before frying.

For deep frying

Place 4-inches of vegetable oil in a pot and heat to 350°F. Carefully place 1 frappe at a time into the oil. It should immediately sizzle up and almost double in size. As soon as it is lightly coloured on all sides, remove from the oil with a slotted spoon and place upside down on a paper towel lined pan. Be careful not to stack too many onto each other as they will break apart.

Once they are cooled and you are ready to serve them, sprinkle lightly with icing sugar and arrange on a platter.

FROLLINI AL BURRO

FROLLINI AL BURRO, OR ITALIAN BUTTER COOKIES, ARE A CLASSIC IN ANY BAKERY. THEY ARE TYPICALLY SHAPED INTO SHELLS, FLOWERETTES, AND LADY FINGERS AND TASTEFULLY DECORATED. FOR THE HOME BAKER, A COOKIE PRESS WORKS GREAT AND IS EASY ENOUGH FOR KIDS TO USE TOO. A GREAT COOKIE FOR SANDWICHING TOGETHER WITH JAMS OR CHOCOLATE.

1 cup (250 mL) unsalted room temperature butter

1 ⅓ cup (330 mL) icing sugar

3 large eggs

2 tsp (10 mL) vanilla extract

3 ¼ cup (810 mL) all-purpose flour

pinch of salt

Preheat oven to 375°F.

Prepare baking sheets. You can use parchment paper, but we found that it is actually easier to shape the cookies on a bare pan.

Make sure the butter is at room temperature.

Beat the butter until soft and fluffy. Add the icing sugar and continue to beat for 5-10 minutes until it resembles a thick whipped cream.

Add the eggs and vanilla and beat for another 5 minutes.

Sift the flour into a bowl and add to the mixture a little at a time while mixing on low speed.

Once flour is incorporated, add the salt and give a final little mix.

Use a piping bag to shape cookies into classic fingers, rosettes, or shells, or use a cookie press to make shapes as in the picture.

Bake for 15 minutes or until they just start to turn golden. Let sit for a couple of minutes and then transfer to a baking rack.

Once cooled completely, you can decorate as you wish.

OPTIONAL

To make the different coloured cookies, simply add a few drops of the desired food colouring to the cookie dough.

LEMON ANGINETTI

Lemon anginetti, also known as lemon twists, lemon drop cookies, or Italian knot cookies, are easy to make and have a great lemon flavour. You will find these at most celebrations often decorated with coloured sprinkles.

½ cup (125 mL, 95 g) vegetable shortening

½ cup (125 mL) granulated sugar

3 large eggs

1 ½ tsp (7.5 mL) pure lemon extract

zest and juice of 1 lemon

3 cups (750 mL) all-purpose flour

2 tsp (10 mL) baking powder

pinch of salt

For the glaze

1 cup (250 mL) icing sugar

4 ½ tsp (22.5 mL) lemon-flavoured liqueur

4 ½ tsp (22.5 mL) lemon juice

zest of 1 lemon

Preheat oven to 350°F.

Prepare baking sheets lined with parchment paper.

Beat the vegetable shortening and sugar in a large mixing bowl. Add the eggs, one at a time, beating in between. Once the eggs are incorporated, add the lemon extract, lemon juice, and lemon zest.

In a separate bowl blend together the flour, baking powder, and salt. Add the dry ingredients a little at a time to the mixture. Once combined, the mixture should be soft and sticky.

To form the cookies, use a tablespoonful of dough and roll it to a 6-inch long log. Bend it in half and gently twist a couple times. Lightly pinch the ends to seal.

Place the cookies onto the baking sheet.

Bake for 10-12 minutes. They will still be very light in colour when cooked. Transfer to a baking rack.

For the glaze

Prepare the glaze by combining all the ingredients in a bowl and whisk until smooth. Brush over the tops of the cookies and let dry.

OPTIONAL

Instead of twist shapes you can also make these into drop cookies. Use a tablespoon of dough and roll into a ball before baking.

MEZZA LUNA

A HALF-MOON COOKIE WITH A RICH FILLING. THE TRADITIONALLY USED "MOSTOCOTTO" IS REPLACED WITH GRAPE JAM IN THIS FAMILY RECIPE AND GIVES IT A WONDERFUL UNIQUE FLAVOUR.

For the filling

2 cups (500 mL) grape jam

2 tsp (10 mL) cocoa powder

zest of 1 orange

¾ cup (185 mL, 112 g) chopped almonds

½ cup (125 mL) brewed espresso coffee

1 tsp (5 mL) vanilla extract

1 tsp (5 mL) ground cinnamon

½ cup (125 mL) granulated sugar

1 cup (250 mL) fine bread crumbs

For the dough

4 large eggs

4 tsp (20 mL) baking powder

zest of 1 Lemon

2 cups (500 mL) granulated sugar
(plus extra for sprinkling)

1 cup (250 mL) vegetable oil

½ cup (125 mL) milk

½ cup (125 mL) water

1 package vanillina

6 cups (1500 mL) all-purpose flour plus 1 extra cup (250 mL) set aside for use while kneading

For the filling

Place the jam in a pot on medium heat and stir constantly. Add all the ingredients, except for bread crumbs, and bring to a boil.

Once it begins to boil, add the breadcrumbs and continue cooking at a boil for an additional 2 minutes. If you find it too runny either add more bread crumbs or more almonds.

Place in a bowl and let stand overnight in the refrigerator or up to 1 week.

For the dough

Preheat oven to 350°F.

Prepare a baking sheet lined with parchment paper.

Mix eggs, baking powder, lemon zest, sugar, oil, milk, water, and vanillina in a bowl. Gradually add the flour. Transfer the dough to a lightly floured work surface. Knead by hand, using some of the extra flour if needed, just until it no longer sticks to your hands.

Roll the dough to a ⅛-inch thickness and use a 4-inch round cookie cutter to cut out circles. Place 1 ½ teaspoonfuls of filling in the middle of each circle, fold over and use a fork to seal the edges.

Place on the baking sheet and bake for 15 minutes or until golden brown.

OPTIONAL

Before baking, brush the tops with an egg white wash and sprinkle with granulated sugar.

MOSTACCIOLI

MOSTACCIOLI ARE A COMMON COOKIE IN SOUTHERN ITALY AND ARE A TRADITIONAL CHRISTMAS TREAT. A SPICED COOKIE WITH A SWEET GLAZE THAT PAIRS AMAZINGLY, OF COURSE, WITH A HOT ESPRESSO.

For the dough

2 cups (500 mL) honey

1 cup (250 mL) granulated sugar

2 large eggs

zest and juice of 1 orange

1 tsp (5 mL) ground cinnamon

pinch of baking powder

pinch of baking soda

3 cups (750 mL, 454g) almonds
(roasted and finely chopped)

2 cups (500 mL) all-purpose flour

For the glaze

2 Tbsp (30 mL) water

2 cups (500 mL) icing sugar

1 Tbsp (15 mL) orange juice

1 Tbsp (15 mL) orange-flavoured liqueur (optional or replace this volume with more orange juice)

Preheat oven to 350°F.

Prepare a baking sheet lined with parchment paper.

Mix the honey, sugar, eggs, orange zest, orange juice, cinnamon, baking powder, and baking soda together until well blended.

Combine the almonds and flour together and add to the wet ingredients. Mix together to form a dough.

Cover with food-safe plastic wrap and place overnight in the refrigerator.

On a lightly floured surface, roll out ¼ of the dough at a time into a 3-inch wide rectangle and ¼-inch in thickness. Cut into diamond shapes.

Place cookies onto the baking sheet and bake for about 15 minutes or until lightly coloured.

Let cool completely before glazing.

For the glaze

Prepare the glaze by adding the water to the icing sugar and stir until it is smooth and there are no lumps. Add the orange juice and liqueur if using and mix well.

Spoon a bit of the glaze onto a cookie and use the back of the spoon to spread it evenly over the surface.

You want the glaze to spread easily but not drip off the cookie. You can adjust the consistency either by adding small increments of icing sugar if too runny or water if too thick.

Place the glazed cookies on a baking rack set over a pan or piece of parchment paper to catch any drippings. Let them sit for a few hours to allow the glaze to set.

Store in an airtight container in a cool place.

MOSTACCIOLI 2

THIS VARIATION OF MOSTACCIOLI IS SOFT AND CHOCOLATEY. ROASTED ALMONDS WITH CHOCOLATE AND ESPRESSO...SAY NO MORE!

For the dough

¼ cup (60 mL) milk

¼ cup (60 mL) prepared espresso

⅔ cup (165 mL, 125 g) semi-sweet chocolate

1 cup (250 mL) cocoa powder

1 ½ cups (375 mL) granulated sugar

2 large eggs

¼ cup (60 mL, 50 g) shortening

2 cups (500 mL) all-purpose flour

250 g roasted almonds finely ground

pinch of cinnamon

pinch of ground cloves

1 ½ tsp (7.5 mL) ammonium bicarbonate for baking (dissolved in 3 tablespoons of warm milk)

For the glaze

2 cups (500 mL) icing sugar

4-5 Tbsp (60-75 mL) milk

Preheat oven to 350°F.

Prepare a baking sheet lined with parchment paper.

In a small pot, mix together the milk, espresso, chocolate, cocoa, and sugar. Stir over low heat until everything is melted.

Beat the eggs in a separate bowl.

Melt the shortening separately over low heat.

In a large bowl, stir the flour and almonds together. Add to this the chocolate mixture along with the eggs, melted shortening, cinnamon, ground cloves, and ammonium bicarbonate mixture. Mix until a dough forms. The dough should not stick to your hands.

Transfer the dough onto a large, lightly floured work surface. Cut small portions of the dough at a time and roll lengthwise into a 1-inch diameter by ¼-inch thick log. Flatten the tops lightly with your hands and cut on a diagonal to form diamond shapes about 2 inches wide.

Place on the baking sheet and bake for 12 minutes.

For the glaze

Add only enough milk to dissolve the icing sugar.

Brush on top of cookies when almost cooled.

TIPS
Ammonium bicarbonate is available in the baking aisle of most grocery stores.

MOSTOCCIOLI CALABRESE

CALABRESE MOSTACCIOLI, OR "MA-STRU-ZOLO" IN DIALECT, ARE A TRADITIONAL SOUTHERN ITALIAN COOKIE. A SUPER QUICK AND EASY RECIPE WITH VERY FEW INGREDIENTS. TRADITIONALLY YOU WOULD FIND THESE AROUND CHRISTMAS MADE INTO ELABORATE SHAPES AND DESIGNS. THIS BISCOTTI STYLE COOKIE IS SIMPLE TO MAKE.

1 cup (250 mL, 150 g) whole almonds

3 cups (750 mL) all-purpose flour

¾ cup (185 mL) granulated sugar

1 Tbsp (15 mL) baking soda

½ cup (125 mL) honey

1 ½ tsp (7.5 mL) vegetable oil

½ cup (125 mL) water

Preheat oven to 350°F.

Prepare a large baking sheet lined with parchment paper.

Roast the almonds for about 5 minutes or until fragrant.

In a large bowl stir together the roasted almonds, flour, sugar, and baking soda.

Combine the honey, vegetable oil, and water in a separate bowl and mix well.

Add the wet ingredients to the flour and nut mixture and mix by hand until well combined.

Turn onto a lightly floured surface and knead gently to form a dough that is very soft.

Split into two equal parts and form each into a log about two inches high.

Place in the center of the oven and bake for 35 minutes or until dark brown.

Let cool for 20 minutes before cutting into strips.

OPTIONAL
You can omit the sugar by adding another ½ cup of honey and cutting the water down to ¼ cup.

NOCHETTE

A simple pastry dough with a rich dollop of flavour packed into bite-sized cookies. It's hard to say if the dough or the filling is the star here, but they work so well together, there's no need to pick!

For the filling

2 cups (500 mL) prune jam

4 tsp (20 mL) cocoa powder

9 Tbsp (135 mL) granulated sugar

zest of one lemon

zest of one orange

1 tsp (5 mL) ground cinnamon

1 cup (250 mL) finely chopped almonds

⅓ cup (80 mL) fine bread crumbs

For the dough

3 ½ cups (875 mL) all-purpose flour

4 eggs

1 cup (250 mL) granulated sugar

4 tsp (20 mL) baking powder

1 pkg vanillina

zest of one lemon

1 cup (250 mL) unsalted room temperature butter

1 egg for egg wash

For the filling

Place the jam in a pot on medium heat, stirring constantly. Add all the filling ingredients, except for the bread crumbs, and bring to a boil.

Once it begins to boil, add the breadcrumbs and continue cooking at a boil for an additional 2 minutes. If you find it too runny, either add more bread crumbs or more almonds.

Place in a covered bowl and let stand overnight or up to 1 week in the refrigerator.

For the dough

Preheat oven to 350°F.

Prepare a baking sheet lined with parchment paper.

Mix all the ingredients together in a bowl. Turn onto a lightly floured work surface and knead by hand to form a dough. Separate the dough into 4 equal portions and cover in food safe plastic wrap. Refrigerate for 1 hour.

Roll out the dough to approximately ⅛-inch thick and cut into 2-inch squares. Place a small amount of filling from corner to corner diagonally then bring over the opposite two corners and pinch together to seal in the middle.

Place on the baking sheet, brush with the egg wash and bake for 10 minutes or until golden.

PASTA FROLLA THUMBPRINTS

PASTA FROLLA, OR SHORTCRUST, IS A GREAT BASIC COOKIE DOUGH AND IS THE BASE FOR SO MANY OTHER GREAT ITALIAN DESSERTS. THIS IS A RECIPE YOU DEFINITELY WANT TO HAVE IN YOUR BAKING REPERTOIRE! WE HAVE TAKEN ONE OF OUR NONNA'S RECIPES AND ADAPTED IT TO THIS THUMBPRINT COOKIE THAT WE KNOW YOU WILL LOVE!

4 extra-large egg yolks

1 ½ cups (375 mL) icing sugar

1 ¼ cup (310 mL) room temperature butter (cut into small pieces)

3 cups (750 mL) all-purpose flour

juice of ½ lemon

1 tsp (5 mL) vanilla extract

pinch of salt

preserves for filling

In a mixing bowl, cream together the egg yolks and icing sugar. Add the butter and half of the flour. Mix together to incorporate. Add the remaining flour and mix again.

Add the lemon juice, vanilla extract, and salt. Mix to combine then transfer to a lightly floured work surface and gently knead by hand to form a smooth dough. Cover with food-safe plastic wrap and refrigerate for 1 hour.

Preheat oven to 350°F and prepare a baking sheet lined with parchment paper.

Remove the dough from the refrigerator and place on a lightly floured work surface.

Cut the dough into quarters and roll each piece into a 14-inch log. Cut into 1-inch pieces and roll each into a ball.

Use a dowel or your thumb to make an indent in the center of each ball of dough.

Place on the baking sheet and put half a teaspoonful of your favorite preserve into each indent.

Bake for 12 minutes or until very lightly golden.

OPTIONAL

Instead of thumbprints, you can roll out the dough to ½-inch thick and use cookie cutters to make your favourite shape cookies.

PASTARELLE

A VERY OLD, AND TRADITIONAL RECIPE BUT THERE IS SOMETHING FANTASTIC ABOUT THIS SIMPLE COOKIE. OFTEN ENJOYED AT BREAKFAST OR AS A SNACK WITH A COFFEE. THE SUGAR SPRINKLED ON TOP GIVES THEM THE PERFECT BIT OF CRUNCH.

6 large eggs

zest of 1 lemon

1 cup (250 mL) vegetable oil plus extra to coat bowl and hands

2 cups (500 mL) granulated sugar

1 tsp (5 mL) vanilla extract

¼ cup (60 mL) milk

2 Tbsp (30 mL) baking powder

6 ½ cups (1625 mL) all-purpose flour plus ½ cup (125 mL) to sprinkle on work surface

1 egg for egg wash

granulated sugar for sprinkling

Preheat oven to 350°F.

Prepare a baking sheet lined with parchment paper.

In a large bowl, whisk together the eggs, lemon zest, oil, sugar, vanilla, and milk.

In a separate bowl, stir the baking powder and flour together. Add this into the wet ingredients and work together until a dough is formed.

Transfer the dough onto a lightly floured work surface and gently knead it to the point where it does not stick to your hands. Form into a ball and place into a large bowl that has been lightly coated with vegetable oil.

Let the dough rest for about 5 minutes.

Lightly coat your hands with oil and take a small piece of dough at a time, slightly smaller than a golf ball. On a floured work surface, roll it into a log 9-inches by ⅜-inch.

Start forming the cookie with 1-inch of the log standing upright in the center and spiralling the rest of the log around it. It helps to hold the center piece with one hand while you are doing this.

Place on the baking sheet. Brush the tops of each cookie with egg wash and sprinkle lightly with sugar.

Bake for 15 minutes or until nicely coloured.

PASTE DI MANDORLE

THESE COOKIES AREN'T JUST KNOWN FOR THEIR GOOD LOOKS! SO FEW INGREDIENTS, YET THESE SOFT AND SOMEWHAT CHEWY COOKIES ARE SO DELICIOUS AND BURSTING WITH ALMOND FLAVOUR.

2 cups (500 mL, 300 g) whole almonds

2 cups (500 mL) icing sugar, lightly packed

2 extra-large egg whites

½ teaspoon (2.5 mL) pure almond extract

maraschino cherries for topping

Prepare a baking sheet lined with parchment paper.

To prepare the almonds, bring a small pot of water to a boil and drop the almonds in for 1 minute. Remove the almonds and place on a tea towel. Remove skins by pinching each almond between two fingers. The skins will come off easily. Once finished, roast the almonds in the oven for a few minutes to dry completely.

Once the almonds are dry, use a food processor to finely grind the them into a flour.

Add the icing sugar and mix again to make sure it is well combined and very fine.

In a bowl, whisk together the egg whites and almond extract.

With the food processor on, add the egg white mixture slowly. The dough will come together quickly and be very soft.

Prepare a pastry bag with a large star tip and fill with the dough.

Pipe the cookies directly onto the baking sheet. Rosettes and seashells are the most common shapes.

Place a cherry or almond into the center of the cookie.

Let the prepared cookies rest in a cool place while the oven heats up to 400°F.

Bake for 8 minutes or until just the edges start to brown. The center of the cookie should remain soft and chewy.

Let cool for 10-15 minutes and transfer to a baking rack to cool completely.

TIPS

Wetting the inside of the pastry bag with water prevents the dough from sticking to the bag. You can let the prepared cookies rest overnight and then bake for just 4-5 minutes at 400°F. The extended rest allows them to dry a little so they don't flatten and adds to the texture of the cookie.

PESCHE

IT WAS GREAT TO FINALLY RECORD THE RECIPE FOR THESE "PEACHES". THESE ARE ALWAYS A FAVOURITE AND MAKE A VERY IMPRESSIVE DESSERT TRAY AT PARTIES AND CELEBRATIONS. THE COLOUR MIXTURE HAS JUST THE RIGHT AMOUNT OF LIQUOR, AND THE DELICATE TEXTURE OF THE DOUGH COMBINED WITH THE FILLING MAKES THEM DIFFICULT TO RESIST.

For the filling

1 package of
vanilla instant pudding

For the cookies

2 large eggs

½ cup (125 mL) granulated sugar

⅓ cup plus 2 tsp (90 mL) vegetable oil

2 tsp (10 mL) baking powder

2 cups (500 mL) all-purpose flour

For the colour mixture

½ cup (125 mL) red vermouth

2 Tbsp (30 mL) rum

¼ cup (60 mL) water

red food colouring (colour to your preference)

granulated sugar for rolling

Prepare 1 package of vanilla instant pudding as per package directions and refrigerate.

Preheat oven to 350°F.

Prepare a baking sheet lined with parchment paper.

In a large bowl, mix the eggs and sugar together until well blended. Add in the oil and mix well.

Add the baking powder and flour and mix until all incorporated.

Transfer to a lightly floured work surface and gently knead the mixture until it no longer sticks to your hands. Add a little more flour if needed.

Roll into little balls slightly smaller than golf balls. Use a measuring spoon to make them consistent.

Place on the baking sheet and bake for 13 minutes.

Allow the cookies to cool.

Remove a small scoop from the center of each cookie on the flat side. Do not pierce through to the outside of the cookie. Fill the hole with vanilla pudding and match two cookies together to form a peach.

In a small bowl, mix together all of the colour mixture ingredients.

Sprinkle a generous amount of sugar onto a flat plate.

Roll each peach into the colour mixture and then in the granulated sugar.

Arrange on a tray. Cover and refrigerate until ready to serve.

OPTIONS
As an option you can try the cannoli cream on page 48-49 as a filling.

PIZZELLE

PIZZELLE ARE A THIN WAFER COOKIE WITH A DELICATE FLAVOUR AND CRISP TEXTURE. THE BATTER ONLY TAKES A MINUTE TO WHIP TOGETHER, SO THIS IS THE QUICKEST COOKIE YOU'LL EVER MAKE! PIZZELLE IRONS COME IN A VARIETY OF DECORATIVE PATTERNS AND ARE VERY SIMPLE TO USE.

3 large eggs

½ cup (125 mL) granulated sugar

½ cup (125 mL) room temperature butter

1 ½ tsp (7.5 mL) baking powder

1 ¼ cups (310 mL) all-purpose flour

zest and juice of ½ lemon

juice of ½ orange

1 ½ tsp (7.5 mL) vanilla extract

In a large bowl, mix together all the ingredients and whisk well.

Preheat the pizzelle iron per manufacturer's instructions.

Each pizzelle maker is different, so it is important to refer to their recommendations for quantity of batter to use and how long to cook.

These pizzelle are golden in colour and crunchy when cooled.

Do not freeze. Store in an airtight container.

OPTIONAL

For a variation, try substituting the vanilla with an ounce of anise extract. Also, pizzelle can be formed into ice cream cones or cups, but you've got to be quick! As soon as you take them off the iron, try your hand at forming them.

PIZZELLE DI PRATOLA PELIGNA

THESE ITALIAN WAFFLE COOKIES ARE WONDERFULLY FRAGANT AND NOT TOO SWEET. THEY ARE GREAT ON THEIR OWN, OR YOU CAN TOP THEM WITH A BIT OF JAM AS AN EXTRA TREAT. YOU WILL NEED A STOVE-TOP PIZZELLE IRON TO MAKE THESE COOKIES (SEE NOTES BELOW).

2 cups (500 mL) granulated sugar

12 large eggs

zest of 1 lemon

1 cup (250 mL) melted butter

¼ cup (60 mL) anisette liqueur (secret ingredient!)

7 ½ cups (1875 mL) all-purpose flour

4 tsp (20 mL) baking powder

juice of 1 lemon

In a large bowl, beat the sugar and eggs with a mixer on high for 2 minutes. Add the lemon zest and mix for another minute. Add the melted butter, scrape down the sides of the bowl, and mix for 2 more minutes. Add the anisette and mix to incorporate all the ingredients.

Add 5 ½ cups of flour to the bowl, one cup at a time, kneading with your hands in between. Add the baking powder and lemon juice to the batter and continue to knead with your hands.

Spread 1 cup of flour onto a work surface and transfer the batter onto it. As you gently knead the dough, work the remaining flour into it, half a cup at a time, until it no longer sticks to your hands. The dough should be soft like pizza dough. You may not need to use all of the remaining 2 cups of flour.

Bring together into a large round ball and place into an oiled bowl.

Let it rest for 10 minutes while the pizzelle iron heats up to a medium heat on stove-top burners

With a floured knife, cut the dough into 12 equal pieces.

One at a time, form each of the 12 pieces into a log about 24 inches long and then cut each of the logs into 7 equal pieces. Roll each of the 7 pieces into an 18-inch log and form a figure-8 shape.

Put each figure-8 onto a clean cloth. Place one at a time onto the heated pizzelle iron. Close tightly and flip right away onto the other side. Open the lid to check, and when slightly coloured, flip again.

When both sides are done, about 4 minutes in total, carefully remove the cooked pizzelle and place onto a baking rack to cool.

NOTES

If you don't have a stove-top iron, an electric waffle iron will do the trick!

Work only some of the dough at a time and keep the remainder covered with food-safe plastic wrap to keep it from drying out. When rolling the dough into the logs, sprinkle small amounts of flour onto the work surface if needed to keep the dough from sticking.

PROFITEROLES AND CREAM PUFFS

An easy-to-make choux pastry filled with an Italian pastry cream. Bite-sized profiteroles or larger sized cream puffs are great for a special dessert.

For the pastry

1 cup (250 mL) water

½ cup (125 mL) butter or margarine

½ teaspoon (2.5 mL) salt

1 Tbsp (15 mL) granulated sugar

1 cup (250 mL) all-purpose flour

4 large eggs

For the cream filling

1x250 g package of room temperature cream cheese

1 cup (250 mL) fruit sugar

1 tsp (5 mL) pure vanilla extract

1 tsp (5 mL) grated lemon zest

2 tsp (10 mL) lemon juice

1 cup (250 mL) whipped dessert topping

icing sugar for dusting

Preheat oven to 400°F.

Prepare a baking sheet lined with parchment paper.

Bring water, butter (or margarine), salt, and sugar to a boil in a medium pot. Add the flour all at once and turn the heat to medium-low. Stir continuously with a wooden spoon until the dough comes away from the pan then remove from heat. Transfer to a mixing bowl and let cool a bit.

Once cooled, add the eggs one at a time and mix to combine between additions. The dough is done when it appears glossy.

Use two teaspoons or a piping bag to form the pastries. Make little mounds 1 ½-inches wide and 1-inch high for profiteroles and about double the size for cream puffs. They will puff out, so be sure to leave space between them. Bake for 25 minutes or until lightly browned. Turn off the oven and let them sit for another 10 minutes to dry. Let cool completely.

For the cream filling

To prepare the cream filling, beat the cream cheese and sugar together in a mixing bowl. Add the vanilla extract, lemon zest, and lemon juice. Mix until well blended. Fold in the whipped dessert topping with a spatula. Refrigerate until ready to use.

Cut each pastry in half and fill with the cream cheese filling. Dust with icing sugar just before serving.

OPTIONAL

You can also fill these with simple whipped cream, ice cream, or even one of the other cream recipes in this book (page 48-49). Try them out and see which is your favourite!

ROSE DEL DESERTO

THESE ARE A SOFT BUTTERY COOKIE WITH A CRISPY COATING THANKS TO THE CORN FLAKES. THEY RESEMBLE DESERT ROSES, HENCE THE NAME. THE HINT OF VANILLA FLAVOURING IS PERFECT IN THIS COOKIE, AND THE ICING SUGAR IS A MUST!

3 large eggs

1 ¼ cups (310 mL) granulated sugar

1 ⅛ cups (280 mL) room temperature butter

1 package vanillina

1 package vanilla-flavoured Italian baking powder

3 ⅓ cups (830 mL) all-purpose flour

corn flakes for rolling

icing sugar for sprinkling

Preheat oven to 350°F.

Prepare a baking sheet lined with parchment paper.

Cream together the eggs, sugar, and butter in a large mixing bowl. Mix in the vanillina and the vanilla-flavoured Italian baking powder.

Add the flour, a little at a time, until all incorporated.

Place corn flakes on a large plate. Use a tablespoon to measure portions of dough and roll each one into a ball. Make 6 balls at a time and roll immediately in the corn flakes before the dough dries. Place corn flakes onto the cookies by hand, if need be, to create a more uniform look.

Place on the baking sheet and bake for 10 minutes.

Transfer to a baking rack to cool and sprinkle with icing sugar just before serving.

S-COOKIES

THIS COOKIE IS CRUNCHY BUT ALMOST MELTS IN YOUR MOUTH. THE ALMONDS, ORANGE JUICE, AND WHISKEY WORK SO WELL TOGETHER, MAKING THIS COOKIE A GREAT ACCOMPANIMENT TO A CUP OF COFFEE.

2 tsp (10 mL) baking powder

½ cup (125 mL) orange juice

2 cups (500 mL) unsalted room temperature butter

1 ½ cups (375 mL) icing sugar

4 Tbsp (60 mL) whiskey

2 large eggs

1 tsp (5 mL) vanillina

1 cup (250 mL, 150 g) roasted almonds, skins removed, finely chopped

1 tsp (5 mL) baking soda

5 cups (1250 mL) all-purpose flour

Preheat oven to 350°F.

Prepare a baking sheet lined with parchment paper.

Combine the baking powder with the orange juice and set aside.

Beat the butter and sugar together until smooth.

Add the whiskey, eggs, vanillina, and the orange juice mixture and mix until well blended.

Add the almonds and blend thoroughly.

Add the baking soda to the flour and whisk to mix. Slowly add this to the almond mixture until well incorporated and a dough forms.

Dust a small amount of icing sugar onto a work surface. Take a small amount of dough at a time and roll into ½ inch by 6 inch logs. Form the logs into an "S" shape and place on the baking sheet.

Be sure to space well, as they expand during baking.

Bake for 13 minutes or until golden in colour. Carefully roll them in icing sugar while still warm.

SAVOIARDI

These cookies are also referred to as "lady-fingers". They are commonly used when making tiramisu and other layered desserts. With their slightly crisp texture on the outside but soft and airy consistency on the inside, they make a great treat with a cup of espresso in the middle of the afternoon too!

5 large eggs

1 ⅓ cup (330 mL) granulated sugar

1 tsp (5 mL) pure vanilla extract

1 cup (250 mL) vegetable oil

5 tsp (25 mL) baking powder

5 ⅔ cups (1400 mL) all-purpose flour

icing sugar for rolling

Preheat oven to 350°F.

Prepare a baking sheet lined with parchment paper.

In a large bowl, place the eggs, sugar, vanilla, oil, and baking powder and mix well with an electric mixer.

Add the flour a little at a time, mixing after each addition until it is all incorporated.

Sprinkle icing sugar onto a work surface.

Take a tablespoonful of dough with one spoon and with another spoon scrape the dough down into the icing sugar.

Roll and shape the dough into a log about 3-inches by 1-inch. Alternatively, you can use a piping bag to form these cookies.

Place the cookies onto the baking sheet and bake for 15-20 minutes or until lightly coloured.

Store in a food safe airtight container.

SCARPONE

IF YOU HAVE TAKEN THE TIME TO MAKE MOSTOCOTTO OR OUR SUBSTITUTE VERSION AS SEEN ON PAGE 46, YOU ALREADY KNOW THE UNIQUE FLAVOUR IT BESTOWS ON ANY RECIPE. HERE IT IS COMBINED WITH CHOCOLATE, WALNUTS, AND CITRUS FOR A TRULY RUSTIC TREAT.

3 Tbsp (45 mL) raisins

juice of half a lemon and half an orange

1 cup (250 mL) all-purpose flour

¼ cup (60 mL) granulated sugar

¼ cup (60 mL) cocoa powder

½ tsp (2.5 mL) baking powder

¼ tsp (1.25 mL) ground cinnamon

⅓ cup (80 mL) semi-sweet chocolate chips

1 Tbsp (15 mL) vegetable oil

1 large egg, beaten

⅓ cup (80 mL) mostocotto (see page 54)

zest of half a lemon and half an orange

1 ½ cups (375 mL) coarsely chopped walnuts

Preheat oven to 350°F.

Prepare a baking sheet lined with parchment paper.

In a small bowl, soak the raisins in the lemon and orange juices and set aside while you prepare the dough.

Combine the flour, sugar, cocoa powder, baking powder, and cinnamon in a large bowl and whisk together.

Prepare the chocolate by melting it in a double boiler.

Make a well in the flour mixture. Add the oil, egg, mostocotto, and citrus zests. Mix lightly with a fork and begin to incorporate with the flour. Continue to mix until you have a crumbly dough.

Add the soaked raisins and juices, the melted chocolate, and the chopped walnuts. Use your hands to mix together until well incorporated. You can add a touch more mostocotto if the dough is too dry and crumbly at this point.

Drop spoonfuls of dough onto the baking sheet.

Bake for 10 minutes and transfer to a baking rack to cool.

STRUFFOLI

THESE DEEP FRIED MORSELS OF DOUGH ARE BATHED IN WARM HONEY THEN ADORNED WITH COLOURFUL SPRINKLES. THEY ARE A FESTIVE TREAT AND ONE TO LOOK FORWARD TO AT CHRISTMAS AND EASTER.

2 cups (500 mL) all-purpose flour

1 package vanillina

pinch of salt

1 tsp (5 mL) granulated sugar

3 large eggs + 1 egg yolk, lightly beaten

1 Tbsp (15 mL) brandy

1 Tbsp (15 mL) grated orange zest

2 Tbsp (30 mL) corn oil

corn oil for deep frying (about 2 cups or 500 mL)

1 cup (250 mL) honey

sprinkles and strips of orange zest to decorate

On a work surface, mix the flour, vanillina, salt, and sugar together and form a well. Add the eggs, brandy, grated orange zest, and oil to the well. Blend in the wet ingredients with your hands.

Begin working the dry ingredients into the wet ingredients and continue mixing until a dough forms.

Lightly knead the dough by hand for about 5 minutes until it is uniform.

Cover the dough with food-safe plastic wrap and let it rest for 1 hour.

Work with small pieces of dough at a time and roll each one out into a ½-inch diameter log. Cut each log into ½-inch pieces.

Heat the oil in a deep non-stick pan until it reaches 350°F.

Gently lower the cut pieces of dough into the oil. Keep moving them around in the oil so they cook on all sides.

Allow them to turn golden brown all over. Remove them from the oil with a slotted spoon and let them drain on a pan lined with paper towels. Continue rolling, cutting, and frying the remainder of the dough. Keep the unrolled dough covered in food-safe plastic wrap.

In a separate deep, non-stick pan, heat the honey to a thinner consistency, being careful not to let it burn. Place all the struffoli into the honey and stir until they are completely coated. Remove with a slotted spoon.

Arrange the honey-coated struffoli on a serving dish. Decorate with coloured sprinkles and thin strips of orange zest.

TIPS
Test the oil with a piece of dough. It should bubble or sizzle as soon as the dough hits the oil. The pieces expand to approximately double in size as they cook.

SWEET TARALLI

THESE TARALLI ARE A LARGE AND IMPRESSIVE COOKIE COVERED IN A SWEET LEMON GLAZE AND DECORATED WITH COLORFUL SPRINKLES. THEY ARE TYPICALLY MADE AS A TREAT FOR EASTER WHERE THE THICK, CRUNCHY COOKIE IS BROKEN INTO CHUNKS AND ENJOYED WITH AN ESPRESSO.

For the dough

pinch of salt

2 ½ cups (625 mL) all-purpose flour

4 large eggs

2 tsp (10 mL) vegetable oil

1 Tbsp (15 mL) sambuca liqueur or brandy

For the glaze

2 cups (500 mL) icing sugar

1 ½ Tbsp (22.5 mL) lemon juice

1 ½ Tbsp (22.5 mL) water

sprinkles for decorating

Preheat oven to 380°F.

Whisk the salt and flour together and make a well on a large work surface.

In a small bowl, mix together the eggs, oil, and liquor and add to the well. Slowly work the flour into the egg mixture, being careful not to break the walls of the well. Once all of the flour has been incorporated and a dough is formed, knead the dough until it is shiny and fairly stiff.

Cover and let rest in a bowl for 15 minutes.

Cut the dough into 2 equal portions. Roll each piece into a log about 2-inches in diameter. Take each log and form into a ring, pinching the ends to seal.

Bring a large pot of water to a gentle boil. Submerge one taralle at a time. To make sure the dough maintains a ring shape use a wooden spoon to gently keep the center circle open. As soon as the taralle rises to the top, remove and place on a clean cloth.

Use a sharp, unserrated knife to lightly score the center all the way around the circumference of each ring.

Place the cooled dough rings directly onto the oven racks and bake for 15 minutes. Lower heat to 350°F and cook for another 15 minutes. Lower the temperature again to 320°F and cook for another 15 mintues. The middle of the taralli should be dry.

Transfer to a baking rack to cool.

For the glaze

In a small bowl mix together the glaze ingredients. Brush or spoon the glaze over each tarallo and add sprinkles while still wet. Place onto a baking rack to dry.

TOASTIES

THESE COOKIES ARE SO SIMPLE TO MAKE AND VERY TASTY WITH JUST THE RIGHT HINT OF ORANGE FLAVOR. THESE COOKIES HAVE A CAKE-LIKE INTERIOR ENCLOSED IN A SLIGHTLY CRISPY, TWICE- BAKED OUTER LAYER.

1 cup (250 mL) granulated sugar

½ cup (125 mL) vegetable oil

½ cup (125 mL) margarine

4 large eggs

zest and juice of 1 orange

2 cups (500 mL) all-purpose flour

4 tsp (20 mL) baking powder

Preheat oven to 350°F.

Butter the sides of a 9-inch by 13-inch pan and line the bottom with parchment paper.

Beat together the sugar, oil, margarine, eggs, orange juice, and zest until well mixed. Add the flour and baking powder and mix for 2-3 minutes until well blended.

Bake for 25-30 minutes.

When the cake is done, take it out of the oven. Lift it out of the pan and place it onto a cutting board.

Cut the cake into 1-inch wide strips and lay them on their side on a baking sheet lined with parchment paper.

Place back into the oven for 10-15 minutes until lightly toasted or golden brown.

When done, remove from the oven, cut into serving size pieces, and cool on a baking rack.

TIP

These are best on the first day, but if they are a few days old you can reheat them in the oven for a few minutes and they will taste like you just made them. They also freeze well. Just pop them into the oven at 250°F for about 15 minutes to warm up.

TORRONCINI

THIS IS ONE OF THE CLASSICS! THE COMBINATION OF ROASTED ALMONDS AND HAZELNUTS MAKES FOR A FLAVOURFUL BISCOTTI. THIS IS A CRUNCHY COOKIE PERFECT FOR DUNKING IN COFFEE.

6 large eggs

3 cups (750 mL) granulated sugar

4 cups (1000 mL) all-purpose flour

2 cups (500 mL, 300 g) roasted almonds

2 cups (500 mL, 300 g) roasted hazelnuts

1 pkg vanillina

1 tsp (5 mL) baking powder

1 cup (250 mL) icing sugar

Preheat oven to 350°F.

Prepare a baking sheet lined with parchment paper.

With an electric mixer, beat the eggs and sugar together for about 20 minutes.

Add the flour a little at a time then add the rest of the ingredients.

Divide the dough into 6 equal portions.

Roll and flatten into logs about 1-inch high and 2-inches wide. If you find the dough is too sticky to handle, add a touch more flour.

Place onto the baking sheet and bake for 35 minutes.

Remove from oven and let cool just slightly. Place onto a cutting board and use a serrated knife to cut the log diagonally making ¾-inch wide slices.

Place them back onto the baking sheet and return to the oven until just coloured on the cut sides.

OPTIONS
This is a classic mixture of almonds and hazelnuts, but you can experiment with other nuts as well. Pistachios are a common and tasty substitute.
These cookies freeze well in an airtight food-safe container.

TORRONE

An Italian nougat treat filled with lightly roasted almonds and hazelnuts that is traditionally found during the Christmas season throughout Italy. This recipe requires a bit of elbow grease but is worth the effort! For this recipe it is important that the ingredients are weighed.

edible wafer paper

3 extra large egg whites

500 g fruit sugar

500 g white honey

2 packages vanillina
(see page 11)

6 cups (1500 mL, 900 g)
whole almonds
(roasted, skins on)

3 ⅓ cups (830 mL, 500 g)
whole hazelnuts
(roasted, skins off)

2 Tbsp (30 mL) almond or
hazelnut-flavoured liqueur
(optional)

Line a 9-inch by 15-inch pan, at least 1-inch deep, with parchment paper so that it is a tight fit on the bottom and sides with a slight overhang on all sides. On top of the parchment paper, place edible wafer paper to fit the exact dimensions of the bottom of the pan. Overlap edges slightly if using more than one piece.

In a large bowl with an electric mixer, beat the egg whites for about 10 minutes until very stiff peaks form. Add ⅓ of the sugar at a time and continue to beat between additions until sugar is dissolved. Beat for at least 2 minutes. Add the honey and vanillina. Combine first with a wooden spoon and then beat with an electric mixer until well mixed. At this point the mixture should be very shiny.

Transfer to a large, heavy-bottom pot. Start cooking over medium heat, and once it starts to bubble, reduce to low heat and cook, stirring constantly, for 30 minutes. Use a wooden spoon to stir, as a spatula will not be strong enough. After 30 minutes the mixture is very smooth and glossy and becomes fragrant.

Add the almonds and hazelnuts and cook while stirring continuously for another 45-60 minutes. The mixture should come away from the sides of the pan to form one big ball and will turn ivory in colour. You will notice the mixture moves as one. It should be tacky and sticky like toffee. If using liqueur, add it during the last 10 minutes of cooking.

Working quickly, and using lightly buttered, large stainless steel spoons, spread the mixture onto the wafer paper-lined pan. Smooth and even out the surface. Cover with a layer of wafer paper. Place a piece of parchment paper on top and use a rolling pin to smooth out the surface. Place a clean tea towel over the parchment paper and place a similar sized pan on top with a heavy weight on it that is evenly distributed such as a case of water or a bag of flour. Let cool like this for about an hour. Remove the weight, tea towel, and parchment paper, and with a large sharp knife, cut the torrone into equal strips.

OPTIONAL

You can use amber honey, but the torrone will be darker in colour. Once prepared and cut into strips, torrone can be stored in the freezer for quite a long period. Wrap it in parchment paper, then foil wrap and place in food-safe freezer bags.

TWIST COOKIES

THIS IS ONE OF OUR MOST HIGHLY REQUESTED RECIPES! THE PREPARATION OF THESE COOKIES WITH ITS FLAKY DOUGH AND SWEET WALNUT FILLING MAKES THEM ABSOLUTELY IRRESISTIBLE.

For the dough

2 cups (500 mL) unsalted room temperature butter

4 cups (1000 mL) all-purpose flour

6 large egg yolks

4 tsp (20 mL) vanilla extract

1 cup (250 mL) sour cream

For the filling

6 large egg whites

3 cups (750 mL) sifted icing sugar

4 cups (1000 mL) finely chopped walnuts

½ cup (125 mL) golden rum

For the dough

Mix the butter into the flour with your hands.

Beat the egg yolks and vanilla extract with a fork and mix into the flour mixture. Add the sour cream and mix together with your hands. Transfer to a lightly floured work surface and knead for about 5 minutes until smooth. Shape into a log. Cover with food-safe plastic wrap and place in the refrigerator overnight.

For the filling

Beat the egg whites until frothy. Add the icing sugar and continue beating until well mixed. Fold in the walnuts and rum if using.

For the assembly

Preheat oven to 350°F.

Prepare a baking sheet lined with parchment paper.

Divide the dough into 7 equal pieces. Keep unused dough covered in the refrigerator. Roll one piece at a time into a 16-inch by 20-inch sheet.

Divide the filling into 7 equal parts and spread 1 part of the filling onto each sheet of dough.

Fold ⅓ of the dough sheet into the middle and then fold the other side over like a letter (see photo on next page).

Each cookie is ¾-inch wide. Make slits lengthwise ¼-inch apart, being careful not to cut through the ends of the cookie on the first two cuts. Make a final cut all the way through to form one cookie. Carefully twist the cookies to shape as in the photo.

Bake on the middle rack until golden brown in colour. Rotate the baking sheet halfway through.

Transfer to a baking rack to cool. Store in an airtight food-safe container. These cookies freeze well.

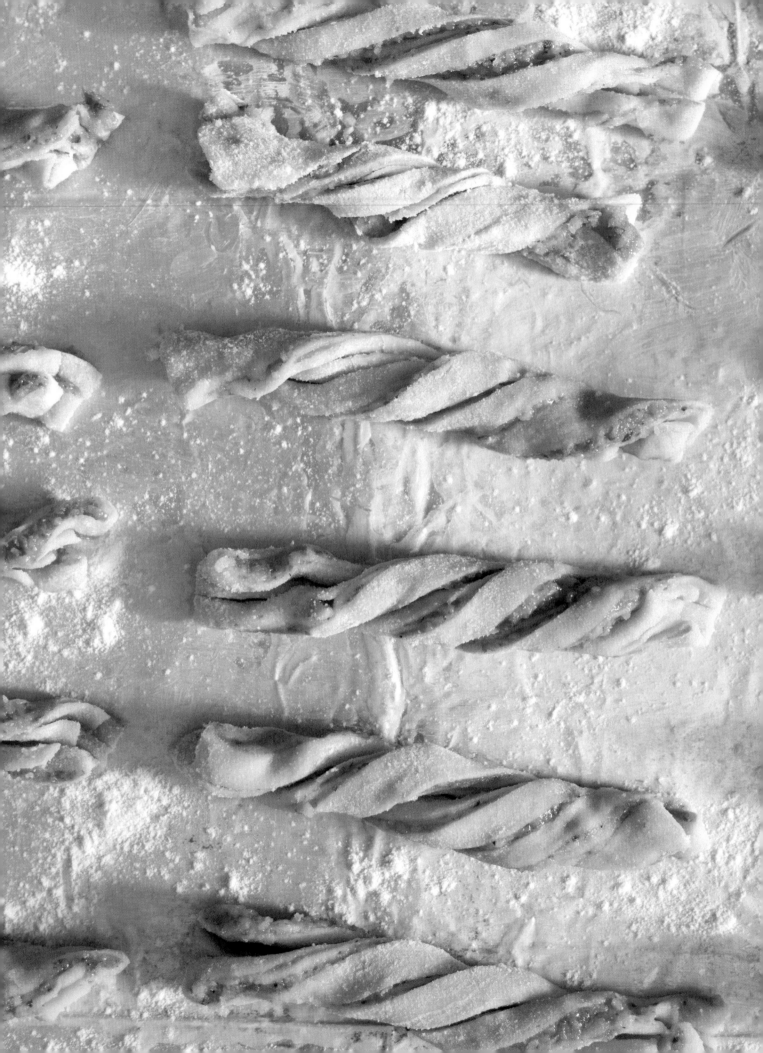

WALNUT DROPS

A SIMPLE BUTTERY, MELT-IN-YOUR-MOUTH COOKIE THAT YOU CAN WHIP UP IN NO TIME AT ALL. THE FINELY GROUND WALNUTS GIVE THIS SHORTBREAD-LIKE COOKIE A GREAT TEXTURE AND DELICATE FLAVOUR.

1 cup (250 mL) unsalted room temperature butter

¼ cup (60 mL) icing sugar

1 tsp (5 mL) pure vanilla extract

2 ¼ cups (560 mL) all-purpose flour

1 cup (250 mL) finely ground walnuts

pinch of salt

maraschino cherries, quartered

icing sugar for rolling

Preheat oven to 375°F.

Prepare a baking sheet lined with parchment paper.

Cream together the butter and icing sugar. Add the vanilla and mix well.

In a separate bowl, combine the flour, walnuts, and salt together. Add to the butter mixture and mix until all incorporated.

Roll the dough into little balls, about 1-inch in diameter or smaller, and press a maraschino cherry quarter into the midde.

Place on the baking sheet and bake for 15 mintues or until lightly coloured on the bottom.

Once cooled, roll the sides of the cookie in icing sugar, trying not to get any onto the cherry.

ZEPPOLE DI SAN GIUSEPPE

A CHOUX PASTRY DOUGH THAT IS BAKED UNTIL LIGHT AND PUFFY THEN FILLED WITH A DELICIOUS VENETIAN CREAM. THEY ARE TRADITIONALLY MADE ON SAINT JOSEPH'S DAY, ONE OF THE MOST RECOGNIZED PATRON SAINT DAYS IN ITALY.

For the venetian cream filling

7 large egg yolks

10 Tbsp (150 mL) granulated sugar

3 ½ cups (875 mL) homogenized milk

1 tsp (5 mL) vanillina

7 Tbsp (105 mL) all-purpose flour

whipped cream or whipped dessert topping

For the pastry

1 cup (250 mL) water

½ cup (125 mL) butter or margarine

½ tsp (2.5 mL) salt

1 Tbsp (15 mL) granulated sugar

1 cup (250 mL) all-purpose flour

4 large eggs

For the filling

Beat the egg yolks, sugar, milk, and vanillina until well blended. Add the flour and continue to beat lightly until all incorporated.

Transfer the mixture to a heavy-bottom sauce pan over medium-low heat. Stir constantly and cook the mixture until thickened and coats the back of a wooden spoon.

Transfer to a glass bowl and cover the surface of the cream with food-safe plastic wrap. Let cool to room temperature and then refrigerate. Just before using, remove from the refrigerator, add a few tablespoonfuls of whipped cream, and gently mix to combine. Adding too much whipped cream will make the filling too runny.

For the pastry

Preheat oven to 375°F. Prepare a baking sheet lined with parchment paper.

In a large, heavy-bottom pot, add the water, butter, salt, and sugar, and bring the mixture to a boil. Next, add the flour all at once. Reduce the temperature to medium and stir constantly until the dough comes away from the sides of the pot. Remove from the heat and transfer to the bowl of an electric mixer.

Let the dough cool slightly and beat in the eggs one at a time. Do not over mix. The dough should be glossy when it is done.

Use a piping bag (we used a Wilton 6B tip) to pipe a circular base of about 2 ½-inches in diameter. Pipe a ring of dough on top, leaving the centre open to form a well for the filling. It should resemble a nest.

Bake for 45 minutes or until well coloured. Transfer to a baking rack to cool. Once completely cooled, fill the center with Venetian cream and sprinkle with icing sugar before serving.

OPTIONAL

This recipe calls for a Venetian cream filling, but other fillings would also work great. For variations see other fillings on page 48-49.

acknowledgements

The making of this book involved the incredible help and support from so many people.

A cookbook is not a cookbook without recipes, so of course we begin by thanking all the contributing nonnas who graciously shared their recipes and kitchen advice.

We had an awesome group of "test kitchen nonnas" who so kindly fielded our questions, physically worked through some of the recipes with us, and who have encouraged us throughout this entire process. A special thank you to Nonna Caterina Imola, Nonna Pina Certo, Nonna Olga Romano, Nonna Anna Polidori, Nonna Sebastiana Oddi, and Nonna Paola Berardi for extending us an open door, a listening ear, and lots and lots of patience!

To our blog followers, it's so nice to know that someone other than our moms loves what we're doing! We look forward to sharing more recipes with you.

So many friends have encouraged us along the way to continue this journey. Your support means so much to us.

Thank you to Jennifer Romano, Erika Polidori, Anna Polidori, Paola Berardi, Chris Laracy, and Carol Imola for helping us to edit the book. Thanks to Ian Beck for guiding us through the printing process, and to Kelly Gyoker for your caricatures that bring smiles to our faces everytime we see them!

To our parents, Pina Certo, Paolo DeSalvo, Caterina & Giovanni Imola, Olga & Pasquale Romano, we deeply admire the courage, strength, and determination it must have taken to embark on a new life in a new country, and we are so grateful that you have carried on and taught us all of your Italian traditions. Your unconditional love and dedication to your family serves as great inspiration as we raise our own families. Thank you for teaching us that hard work and honesty do pay off.

And finally, to our own families, D'Arcy, Paul, Josie, Carmine, Jennifer, and Stefan. Thank you for your patience, advice, and encouragement. You have been force-fed so many cookies and we appreciate your honest feedback! It is such a joy to be able to share this journey with you. Thank you for always believing in us.

about the authors

Angela DeSalvo and Anna Romano are the authors of the food blog Nonna's Way.

We were brought together by a mutual desire to preserve our Italian culture and to share recipes and stories from our mothers, fathers, nonnas, and nonnos. This beloved generation of immigrants serves as a time capsule for us, as they have continued traditions that they brought with them from their homeland of Italy.

We are fiercely proud of our upbringing and heritage and hope to pass this on to our own children and generations to come.

This has been such a wonderful and nostalgic journey for us, and we are happy to share this collection of classic Italian cookies from Nonna's kitchen.

We hope that some of these recipes make it onto your next cookie tray!

We hope that you enjoy this book as much as we have enjoyed putting it together and that it inspires you to not only make the recipes found inside but also to put pen to paper and give your family the gift of generations past to carry forward.

We would love to hear your stories and help you preserve your family's favourite recipes. Share your comments with us at nonna@nonnasway.com.

Visit us at www.nonnasway.com

NONNA'S WAY

THE STORY OF OUR FOOD

A Collection of Classic Italian Cookie Recipes

ANGELA DeSALVO & ANNA ROMANO

Made in the USA
Middletown, DE
27 January 2019